Color

YOUR SCRAPBOOK

PUNCH
ART

MEMORY
MAKERS
BOOKS

Executive Editor Kerry Arquette   **Founder** Michele Gerbrandt

Senior Editor MaryJo Regier

Art Director Andrea Zocchi

Designer Nick Nyffeler

Craft Editor Jodi Amidei

Idea Editor Janetta Wieneke

Photographer Ken Trujillo

Contributing Photographers Marc Creedon, Brenda Martinez, Jennifer Reeves

Contributing Writers Kelly Angard, Julie Labuszewski

Editorial Support Dena Twinem

Hand Model Erikia Ghumm

Featured Artists See Artist Index on page 90

Memory Makers® *Color Your Scrapbook Punch Art*
Copyright © 2003 Memory Makers Books

Published by Memory Makers Books, an imprint of F+W Publications, Inc.
12365 Huron Street, Suite 500, Denver, CO 80234
Phone 1-800-254-9124

First edition. Printed in the United States of America.

10 09 08 07 06 6 5 4 3

Library of Congress Cataloging-in-Publication Data

Color your scrapbook punch art : fun and easy ways to add realistic detail!-- 1st ed.
    p. cm.
  At head of title: Memory makers.
  ISBN-13: 978-1-892127-03-7
  ISBN-10: 1-892127-03-2
    1. Photograph albums. 2. Scrapbooks. 3. Color decoration and ornament--Technique. 4.
  Cut-out craft--Technique. I. Title: Memory makers color your scrapbook punch art. II.
  Memory Makers Books. III. Memory makers.

TR465.C62 2003
745.593--dc21

                                                                                    2003043617

Distributed to trade and art markets by
F+W Publications, Inc.
4700 East Galbraith Road, Cincinnati, OH 45236
Phone 1-800-289-0963

Memory Makers Books is the home of *Memory Makers*, the scrapbook magazine dedicated to educating and inspiring scrapbookers. To subscribe, or for more information, call 1-800-366-6465.
Visit us on the Internet at www.memorymakersmagazine.com

This book belongs to

We dedicate this book to the faithful punch artists featured in this book and to those who
continue to explore and share their fresh, new punch art ideas and techniques.

Table of Contents

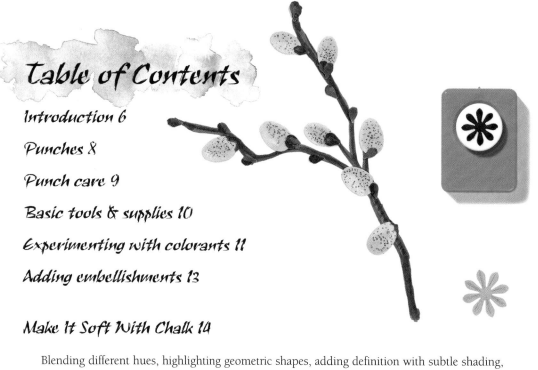

Make It Soft With Chalk 14

Blending different hues, highlighting geometric shapes, adding definition with subtle shading, experimenting with shading techniques, combining with pencil for impact, distressing textured paper, creating depth with intense color on velvet, building roundness and definition, transforming rectangles into curved bamboo, chalking crimped surfaces for texture, crumpling and chalking for a leather look, highlighting pierced designs, enhancing dimensional shapes, brushing to soften edges

Make Your Mark With Pens & Pencils 30

Using contrasting colors for shape definition, accenting a photo mat, creating depth and detail, outlining with whimsical pen strokes, detailing shapes, drawing subtle shadows, creating dimensional flowers, combining shading techniques, giving shapes washed color and shine, brushing watercolor details, mimicking "pointillism," casting light on a pattern, experimenting with pencil shading techniques, daubing shapes for realistic definition, adding artistic effects, adding highlights to distress art, blending for artistic flair, enhancing re-punched shapes, adding highlights, shading layered shapes

Make a Splash With Paint 48

Adding texture with painted backgrounds, adding sizzle to embossed-paper shapes, simulating a snowy scene with stippling, inking and stamping a faux finish, painting and embossing a delicate design, using watercolors to paint a feminine motif, combining colorants for interesting effects, using double-loaded paint for colorful effect, painting and embossing hand-textured shapes, airbrushing vibrant color with ease

Make It Stick With Stamping Inks & Embossing Powders 62

Brushing pearlized powder for an iridescent glow, stamping ornamental designs, enhancing quilt designs with metallic shine, creating texture with embossing powders, emphasizing stamped designs with embossing, embossing a stenciled motif, showcasing an embossed ensemble, impressing letters into embossing enamel, stamping designs into warm embossing enamel, creating faux "hammered tin" accents, highlighting embossed shapes with rub-ons, encapsulating color on "antiqued" glass, adding sparkle and shine to shapes, creating bumpy texture with embossing enamel

Make It Magic With Other Coloring Techniques 76

Revealing color with Scratch-Art® paper, scratching designs to uncover a rainbow of colors, collaging stickers for colorful backgrounds and punched shapes, transferring ink from newsprint for contemporary look, transferring clip art designs onto shapes, rubbing on rich details with metallic leaf, embellishing enameled shapes with detail, layering magazine graphics with punched shapes, embellishing negative space with glass marbles, designing with pressed flowers, coloring punch art with pounded flowers

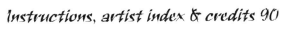

Introduction

An 80th Birthday Surprise

In November of 2002 my grandfather, Tom, turned 80! The whole family had been planning this party for almost 6 months! We managed to keep it a secret...so it really was a big surprise for him. Even his great-grandkids were there... What a terrific chance for them to get to know their great-grandpa!

As punch art continues to expand, Memory Makers continues to experiment and find exciting ways to create with punches. In this book, we show you how to bring your punch art to life with colorants. These are supplies such as pens, chalks, powders and paints that you already have on hand and are using in your scrapbooks.

Color Your Scrapbook Punch Art challenges you to enhance your punch art with a touch of chalk, a few simple pen strokes, a splash of paint, a sprinkle of powder and other magical coloring ideas. We help you discover the distinct characteristics and unique properties of each colorant to enable you to detail your punch art with ease.

Each chapter starts with simple projects and progresses toward more advanced projects, showcasing the innovative and breakthrough work of talented punch artists and coloring experts. Learn how to rub chalk over crimped designs for an elegant emphasis. Experiment with watercolor pencils for a painted effect. Use a loofah sponge, bunched up plastic wrap or bubble wrap to make intriguing textures. Brush on pearl pigment powder over a watermark for an iridescent effect. Transfer newsprint or clip art to your punched shapes with a blender pen for a contemporary look, and so much more.

With the continual introduction and availability of new punches and coloring mediums, the possibilities for creating dynamic punch art become infinite. Use the tips, techniques and insights in this book and marvel at how your punch art evolves with glorious color and rich detail.

Without a doubt, *Color Your Scrapbook Punch Art* will forever change the way you view a punch and your coloring tools and supplies. Enjoy!

Michele

Founder
Memory Makers magazine

Punches

Enter the world of punches and you'll find an enormous selection of shapes, sizes and designs suitable for almost any scrapbook theme. Their versatility and simplicity make them the perfect tool for the beginning scrapbooker, the weekend cropper and the experienced scrapbook pro.

Browse the punch aisle of any scrapbook or craft store and you'll find punches in basic shapes—like a circle, a heart and a diamond. You'll also discover the intricate quilter's block, the classic fleur-de-lis, the seasonal snowflake, the modest teardrop and all the letters of the alphabet. Choose among every size imaginable—from mega to mini!

If you are new to punch art and don't know where to start, begin with a geometric shape, such as a square or a star. Geometric shapes are more versatile than theme-shape punches, such as a dinosaur. Larger-sized punched shapes provide more surface area on which to add color. If you're an experienced punch artist, consider altering the ideas shown using the punches you already have on hand.

Shown below are a few of the punch sizes most widely used in this book. See pages 92-95 for an index of some of the actual punch shapes featured.

Sizes, shapes and colors of punches are approximate and vary slightly between different manufacturers.

Punch care

EXTENDING THE LIFE OF A PUNCH Keep your punch in good working condition with regular maintenance. Every time you sit down to create punch art, bring along a stack of precut 4 x 4" waxed paper and another stack of precut 4 x 4" heavy-duty aluminum foil. Before you begin making punch art, punch through the wax paper (five times) and the foil (another five times) with your punch. The result will be a smooth-working punch and a perfect punched shape. If you don't have foil, a disposable aluminum pie tin works just as well.

REMOVING JAMMED PAPER If paper gets stuck in the punch, place the punch in the freezer for 20 seconds. The metal will contract for easy paper removal. If the punch continues to stick upon the compression, punch through waxed paper five to ten times before using it. This will help the two pieces of metal slide side by side more easily.

CLEANING OFF ADHESIVES Stickers, tape and self-adhesive paper will leave a sticky residue in your punch. Remove with an adhesive remover such as un-du®. Simply squirt the solution on the underside of the punch. Before using, punch through scrap paper until all the solvent has evaporated.

MAKING PUNCH COMPRESSION EASIER Place the punch on a hard, flat surface. Then use the palm of your hand to push down hard. If you need more power, stand up! For repetitive punching, consider using a sturdy and durable punch compression aid like the Power Punch™.

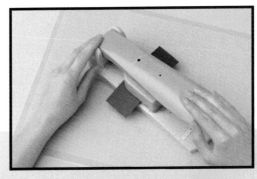

ORGANIZING YOUR COLLECTION Create a quick reference guide by filling a small notebook with each punched shape from your punch assortment. Organize the pages by size, type, or theme. This handy notebook will keep you from purchasing duplicate punches. To quickly identify a punch, punch out the shape in the same paper color as the punch body.

STORING PUNCHES Store your punches covered, in a dry place, to protect against moisture and dust. Plastic bins and large tackle boxes work well for this purpose. Clear containers have the added advantage of visibility. Many companies offer totes and storage containers made specifically for carrying and storing punches. Label your storage containers in the same manner that you label your punch reference guide, if desired.

Basic tools & supplies

Well-maintained punches will create perfect shapes, but what else do you need to make spectacular punch art? The right tools are essential. A craft knife with a fine-point blade used in conjunction with a metal ruler will help you cut straight edges. A cutting mat will protect your work surface. Moist hand wipes will keep hands clean. A paper trimmer comes in handy when cutting large sheets of paper. A pair of tweezers, a piercing tool or a sewing needle aid in picking up and placing small shapes. When using these sharp tools, be sure not to pierce through the paper. Small, sharp scissors work best for precision cutting on punched shapes.

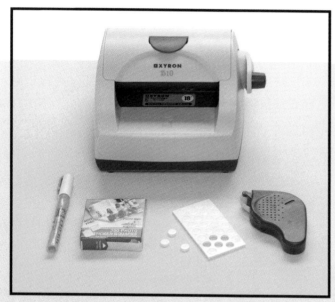

ADHESIVES You have many options for adhering punched shapes to background paper. For small shapes, try a fine-point liquid glue pen. For medium-sized shapes, use a tape roller or photo splits. When working with larger shapes, the Xyron™ machine works well. It coats an adhesive backing onto the paper thereby creating a sticker. Be sure the product you use is considered photo-safe and acid-free.

Selecting paper color

For some artists, selecting paper color comes from the gut—they just know what colors work with their photos. Others find that a color wheel helps with the process. Simply rotate the dial around the spectrum of colors to find harmonious color combinations.

The intense hues of colorants will show up in their purest form on white or light-colored paper. Metallic colorants have a more dramatic effect on black or dark-colored paper. Experiment with colorants on various colored papers to find those that offer the strongest visual impact.

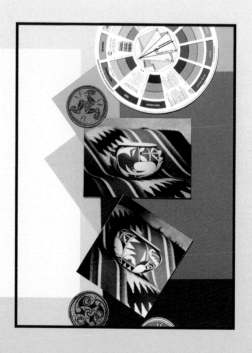

Experimenting with colorants

What exactly is a colorant? According to *Webster's New World™ Dictionary*, a colorant is a pigment, dye, etc., used to give color to something. In the scrapbook world, it's anything that can be used to color your punch art, accent your pages or complement your photos. Most colorants fall into these five categories: chalk, pens and pencils, paint and stamping inks and embossing powders. Many colorants made specifically for scrapbooking are photo-safe. Check with a product manufacturer or your local scrapbook or craft store to be certain.

What's the best colorant to use on punch art? It depends on the look you want to achieve. Experiment with various mediums to understand their distinct characteristics. Learn how to take advantage of their unique properties. Practice different techniques. The supplies you need will depend on the medium you will be applying to your punch art and what effect you want to achieve.

CHALK Add a subtle touch to your punched shapes with colored chalk. Place paper towels atop your work surface when working with chalk. Apply with a cotton ball, cotton swab, makeup sponge, and sponge-tip applicator or clip pen with a small pompom attached. Rub, smudge and blend with your fingertip or color blending tools for a soft velvety tone. Use a chalk eraser to remove misplaced chalk on paper.

PENS AND PENCILS Outline punched shapes with a basic black pen or make highlights with a white gel pen. Add loud intense colors with brush pens or quiet soft colors with colored pencils. Simulate a painter's wash with watercolor pencils and a stroke of a water brush.

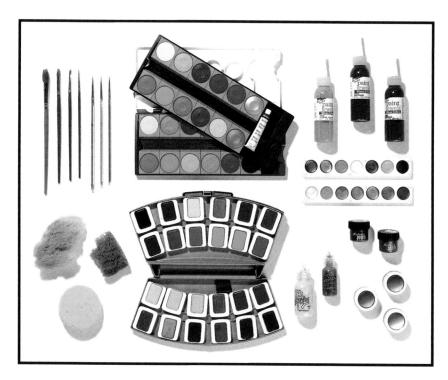

PAINT Brush on translucent watercolor paints for a brilliant wet wash. Use opaque watercolor paints or metallic "rub-ons" for a rich radiant hue. Try pearl, jewel or glitter paints for shimmer and shine. Make gradations in tone or color with a wide brush. Paint on details with a small-pointed brush. Create texture with a firm stippling brush. Daub paint with assorted sponges.

STAMPING INKS AND EMBOSSING POWDERS Stamp punch art with vibrant stamping ink to add interest. Brush on pigment powder on a watermark to fabricate an iridescent glow. Experiment with colored or metallic embossing powders to build a dramatic relief image.

OTHER COLORING IDEAS Experience the magic of Scratch-Art®, the joy of sticker collage and the thrill of transferring ink. Try your hand at the art of flower pounding. Challenge yourself to try these and other coloring ideas for your punch art.

Paper absorption

Take into consideration paper-absorption quality when using colorants. Absorbency refers to the paper's capacity to accept a wet colorant. Glossy paper has little absorbency; therefore a colorant may need to be heat set. Handmade paper has a high absorbency resulting in a colorant bleeding. Most art featured in this book uses cardstock. Prior to coloring your punch art, do a trial run to see how the paper accepts the colorant you are using.

Adding embellishments

The exciting selection of embellishments offers you unlimited possibilities for complementing your colored punch art. Before placing any item on your page, take into consideration these ideas and tips:

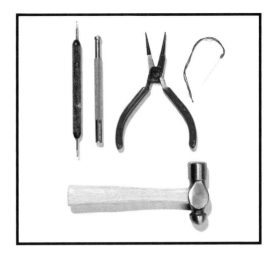

BAUBLES Add an ornamental quality to your punch art with colorful beads, charming buttons, sparkling sequins, flashy rhinestones and playful page pebbles. For example, put sequins on an angelfish shape to create scales, or place a clear page pebble on a splatter shape for a transparent effect. Opt for small, flat objects to avoid adding excess bulk to your album. Strategically place hard embellishments on the page to prevent them from scratching photos on the facing page.

TOOLS FOR APPLYING EMBELLISHMENTS
Embossing stylus, eyelet setter, needle-nose pliers, sewing or embroidery needle and small hammer

METALLICS Give your punch art luster with metallic charms, alluring wire and attractive eyelets. For example, place a charm on a geometric shape to frame it or thread a wire though the top of an ornament shape to add realistic detail. Place all items that may not be photo-safe away from photos.

TEXTILES Dress up your punch art with fancy ribbon, fabulous fiber and decorative thread. For example, attach two mitten shapes with a string of thread or make a tiny ball out of fiber to accompany a cat shape. Test textiles for color permanence. Apply a moist cotton swab to the fabric to see if the dye spreads onto the swab.

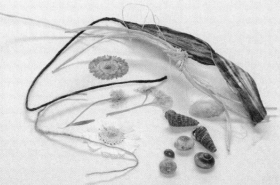

ORGANICS Give your work an organic look with pressed and fresh flowers, dried leaves, natural raffia and tiny shells. For example, turn an ordinary square shape into a glorious gift box by wrapping it in raffia then adding a bow. Plant-based items contain lignin so keep them away from photos.

Make It Soft With Chalk

Let the brilliant pastel tones of chalk delight your senses. You will find the subtle blues, gentle greens and inviting pinks irresistible. Not only is chalk easy to use, but it's a simple way to give a shape dimension.

Create an illusion of roundness to punched shapes by blending different shades of chalk. Experiment with chalk on crumpled or crimped paper for an impressive texture. Rub chalk over crimped designs for elegant emphasis. Smear it over detailed pen work to add interest. Rub it over velvet paper to achieve visual depth.

Cover work surface with paper towel before working with chalk. Apply chalk with a chalk sponge applicator. You can use a cotton ball, a cotton swab or your own finger. Blend and layer colors with a blending tool. Begin with the lightest tone and move to the darkest.

Keep your palette of chalk in good condition. Do not press or twist your applicator into the chalk. Instead, sweep it across the surface. Remove unwanted marks with a chalk eraser. Use spray fixative to preserve your art.

The decorative effects you can achieve with this medium seem endless. Read on to discover how to turn flat circles into ripe oranges, juicy plums and perfect pumpkins.

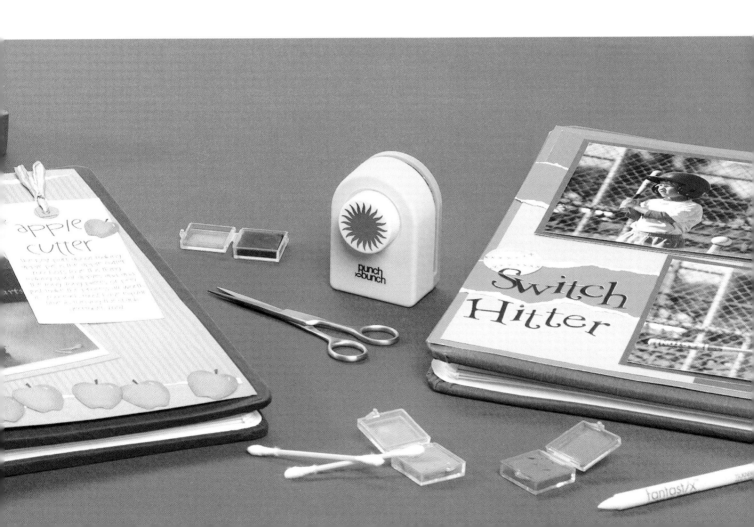

Blending different hues

Blend a rainbow of chalks together on white punched shapes for a soft muted look or intense pop of color depending upon the amount of chalk applied. Follow the punch progression steps below to create the whimsical flowers: Punch heart (All Night Media) for leaves and large pompom (EK Success) for flower from white paper. Lightly shade flower with lavender, pink and orange chalk; blend together well with a clean cotton swab. Embellish with pink rhinestone (The Beadery) at center of flower. Color leaf with heavy strokes of yellow and green chalk for intense color. Mat purple patterned paper with green patterned paper (both Karen Foster Design). Tear strip of solid green paper on two sides; layer vertically over background. Stamp title letters (Hero Arts, Plaid Enterprises) on vellum; cut to size and mount on torn paper strip. Single and double mat photos. Computer print journaling on patterned paper (Magenta) and cut to size. Mount punched flower designs on page with self-adhesive foam spacers. Adhere fibers (Making Memories) along both sides of page.

Pamela Frye

Highlighting geometric shapes

An eye-catching geometric border gets extra pizazz with soft chalk details. Punch large (Punch Bunch) and small (Nankong) triangles from green and yellow papers. Using a cotton swab or dragon clip with a mini pompom attached, brush chalk on two sides of the triangles: green chalk on yellow triangles and yellow chalk on green triangles. Mount triangles close together for a border design. Adhere sentiment sticker (Wordsworth) to complete front of card.

Alexandra Bleicher

Variation

For a simple variation, try these ideas. For the photo frame, alternate medium triangles (Punch Bunch) highlighted with chalk (Craf-T) and 24-gauge silver wire (The Beadery) twisted into scrolls. Adhere wire by leaving a ½" length at the end of wire design, slip into a small hole pierced in paper with a needle, and tape wire end to back of page to secure. For border, mark punch guidelines on back of 1½" wide strip of paper at 1¼" intervals. Insert border strip into upside-down, ¾" circle punch (Marvy/Uchida), center guideline marks and punch. Quarter slice positive circles, chalk and set aside. Punch a second set of circles in coordinating color, slice one-third off of circle, chalk and mount along lower edge of border. Layer quartered circle slices atop two-thirds circles on border. Twist wires into swirls; adhere. Add wire title, matted photos and journaling.

Alexandra Bleicher

Adding definition with subtle shading

Assemble a border of ripe green apples subtly detailed to perfection
with chalk and pen details. Tear patterned paper (EK Success) at top and
bottom; mount on brown paper. Double mat photo. Handcraft tag from
light green paper; attach eyelet to center of punched circle and square.
Finish with paper yarn (Making Memories) tied to tag. Punch medium
and large apples (Family Treasures). Shade around edges with brown
and black chalk. Color stem with black pen; add highlights with white
opaque gel pen. Mount along bottom of page.

Alison Beachem

Experimenting with shading techniques

Give a flat surface dimension and create roundness in an object
by shading the darkest color around the edges of one side of
circle; use the lightest color at the center. Apply medium shades
around the top edges of circle; blend all shades together well.
Follow the punch progression steps below to create the fruit
bowl. Punch large circle (Marvy/Uchida) for bowl from white
speckled paper. Snip off top and bottom of circle as shown.
Add detail to top of bowl with border design punch; layer over
dark brown paper. Add chalk details around edges. Punch
medium circles from orange paper for oranges; shade with
chalk as described above and add pen detail. Layer on background and behind bowl. Double mat completed still life.
Detail the second mat with brown chalk around edges.

Alison Beachem

Combining with pencil for impact

Punched daisies become dimensional sunflowers with the help of pencil and chalk details.
Vertically tear patterned paper (Karen Foster Design); layer over mustard paper. Triple mat photo.
Print journaling; cut to size and wrap with cotton thread (Making Memories). Print title letters;
silhouette cut with craft knife. Follow the punch progression steps below to create sunflowers:
Punch two large daisies (Marvy/Uchida) from golden yellow paper. Emboss lines on each petal
with stylus before adding color with orange pencil. Layer atop one another; apply brown chalk
to outer edges of flower. Mount button (Blumenthal Lansing) at center to complete. Mount
embellished sunflowers on torn tags (Accu-Cut) shaded around the edges with tan chalk.
Tie with cotton floss (DMC) before mounting on page.

Karen Hamlin

Sept. 2001 - Jonah and his
Grandma planted some sunflowers
from a kit that she gave him. We
called them "Jonah flowers". When
the sunflowers bloomed, daddy put
Jonah up high on the fence to take
some photos. And as you can tell,
he was terrified and so proud all at
the same time! First of his
beautiful flowers and second for
being old enough for daddy to put
him on the fence.

Distressing textured paper

Show the natural wear and tear on a well-worn baseball with chalked details lightly rubbed with fine-grain sandpaper. Mat patterned paper (Paper Loft) with orange paper. Tear two horizontal strips of orange paper; mount on page as shown. Mat photos; layer on page. Adhere title sticker letters (Creative Imaginations). Follow the punch progression steps below to create a trio of distressed balls. Punch jumbo circle (Marvy/Uchida) from white textured paper; shade around edges of ball with brown and black chalk. Add stitching lines with red pen (EK Success). Complete distressed look by gently rubbing fine-grade sandpaper over punched design.

Alison Beachem

"Just using brown chalk on the edges can give a punched shape the depth that it needs to stand out."

-Alison Beachem

Creating depth with intense color on velvet

Layer a dramatic border of velvet shapes chalked with vibrant shades of red, orange and gold. Detail all punched shapes with chalk before layering on paper strip to keep velvet free of smudges. Punch jumbo and large squares (Emagination Crafts) from brown velvet paper (Paper Adventures); add gold chalk (Craf-T) over pen stroke details. Punch large squiggles (Emagination Crafts) from light green velvet and gold metallic papers. Color with red and orange chalks before layering atop one another. Punch small primitive hearts (EK Success) from burgundy velvet (Wintech) and gold metallic papers. Layer atop one another and assemble four together in the shape of a flower as shown; add gray and black chalk details to center. Create quasar designs by first punching ¼" circle (EK Success) and then re-punching with mini (Family Treasures) or small (Emagination Crafts) quasar punch. Flip quasar punch over; insert and center punched paper; re-punch with quasar shape. Layer all shapes on strip of black velvet paper (Wintech) punched with lattice border (Fiskars).

Pennie Stutzman

1 Use a cotton swab or fingertips to rub chalk across punched shapes. Use a black journaling pen to add detail lines as shown around the outer edges of each square.

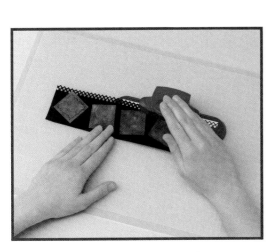

2 Mount detailed squares on a 2½ x 11" black velvet border strip. Insert strip into border punch to create lattice edge. No lining up is needed with this punch; it re-punches where there is any overlap in the design.

> *"Chalking is the easiest medium to work with. It goes on simply, requires no setting or drying time and removes easily if you don't like what you did."*
>
> *-Pennie Stutzman*

Building roundness and definition

Punched and chalk-shaded circles turn into perfectly ripe plums that look as if they were just picked from a tree. Layer purple patterned paper (EK Success) and sliced green paper strip on brown background. Mat photos. Print journaling; cut to size. Add eyelets (American Tag Co.) and fibers (source unknown) to tags (DMD). Adhere title sticker letters (Colorbök). Follow punch progression steps to create plums: Punch medium and large circles (Marvy/Uchida) from light purple paper; brush purple chalk around entire edge of circle. Add a heavy curved line of chalk just off-center from top to bottom. Lightly brush brown chalk along heavy purple chalk line and blend; add pen line down same area. Punch small leaves (EK Success); brush around edges with green chalk. Freehand cut stems from brown paper; layer with leaves on plum.

Alison Beachem

Transforming rectangles into curved bamboo

A little chalk goes a long way when used to shade rectangular shapes to look like curved bamboo segments. Punch medium rectangles (Family Treasures) from tan paper. Trim around rectangle with scissors to round corners and give imperfect edges. Add shading with chalk and detail with pen strokes. Punch medium teardrop (Emagination Crafts) from green suede paper. Brush with dark green chalk for definition. Assemble end-to-end, on an angle as shown; layer with teardrop shapes.

Jenna Beegle

"Coloring punch art is a safe place to play—and one that gives you a lot of impact on your page!"

-Jenna Beegle

Chalking crimped surfaces for texture

It's easy to add detail to crimped, punched shapes by brushing chalk across the crimped "peaks" of the paper. Note how the crimped and receded "valleys" resist the chalk, adding to the illusion of coarseness and grain. To begin, tear two sage green paper border strips; adhere to light olive cardstock for background. Tear photo edges, leaving some edges straight. Print title and journaling onto light green paper; assemble with photos and adhere, overlapping as desired. Adhere fibers (EK Success) along one edge of title and journaling blocks. Follow the steps below to create the punched accents.

Pamela Frye, Photos MaryJo Regier

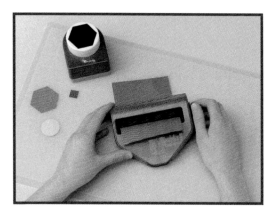

1 Insert paper into crimper (Paper Adventures); roll through the crimper as shown. Repeat with different paper colors as desired. Punch crimped papers with super jumbo hexagon (Emagination Crafts), 1¼" circle (Family Treasures) and small square (Punch Bunch) punches.

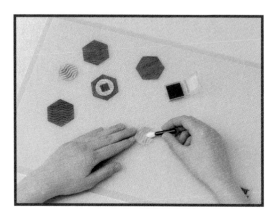

2 Use your fingertip or a sponge-tip makeup applicator to rub black chalk (Craf-T) across the punched shapes. Assemble shapes; adhere to lower edge of page. Repeat both steps using a ½" circle (EK Success) punch to create border across upper edge of page.

Variation

Use this technique to add wood grain to a bare tree (EK Success), bristle to a ponderosa pine cone or saguaro cactus (both Emagination Crafts) or boughs on an evergreen tree (Nankong).

Crumpling and chalking for a leathery look

Moistening, crumpling and then ironing punched shapes adds a vintage leather look to punch art. Use cardstock, however; thinner paper won't hold up to this technique! First rub green chalk (Craf-T) to tag edges; add torn patterned paper (Frances Meyer) and strip of green mulberry paper to tag edges. Attach mulberry square with square eyelet (Making Memories) to tag; thread fibers (On The Surface) through eyelet and knot. Follow the punch progression steps to age and add color: Punch contemporary tree (Emagination Crafts); moisten, crumple and unroll; press (don't rub) shape with iron on cotton setting (no steam); rub chalk across tree and accent with gold pen dots.

Deborah Breedlove

Variations

Try this technique to weather brittle leaves or age some well-handled footballs, too! Leaf tag: jumbo maple and red oak leaf punches (Emagination Crafts), mesh (Magic Scraps), fiber (Wonderland Emporium). Football tag: football punch (Emagination Crafts), eyelets (Making Memories), fiber (On The Surface).

Deborah Breedlove

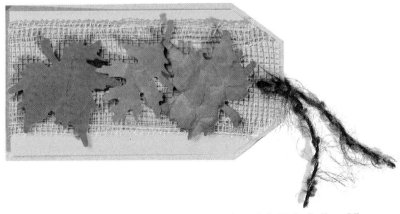

Highlighting pierced designs

An elegant assembly of punched and pierced hearts provides the perfect frame for a quilt-inspired heritage page. Punch three sizes of hearts (Marvy/Uchida) from ivory paper. Use a piercing tool or sewing needle to pierce holes around edges of each heart. Rub tan chalk around heart over pierced holes with cotton swab. Follow the steps on the next page to create pierced background. To create wreath heart, punch 13 tri-leaf (EK Success) shapes from green paper. Punch eight ³⁄₁₆" circles (EK Success) from yellow paper and eight mini flowers (All Night Media) from red paper. Begin assembling heart at bottom point with tri-leaf shape, working up each side simultaneously. Place each piece, end-to-end, layering leaf over stem. Layer mini flowers and circles over leaves as shown. Double mat photo to fit center square; adhere sticker letters (Creative Imaginations).

Jenna Beegle, Photo Jodi Amidei

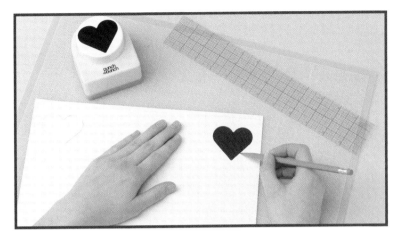

1 Use a ruler and pencil to draw grid lines for 12 x 12" page layout. Draw a border around page ¼" from edge of paper. Draw two vertical lines, 2¾" from side borders and two horizontal lines 2¾" from upper and lower borders. Trace around punched super jumbo heart (Punch Bunch) at each corner to use as a pattern for wreath heart.

"Pierced holes are really only suggestions of shadow. But with chalk, they become a fine detail, like the stitching on an antique quilt that is gently distressed with years of loving use."

-Jenna Beegle

2 Use a piercing tool or sewing needle to pierce on all penciled lines at ¼" intervals.

3 Use a cotton swab to rub chalk across all pierced lines.

Enhancing dimensional shapes

Hang fall's bountiful harvest in seasonal shapes and colors on a dimensional border.

PUMPKIN Punch three large circles (Family Treasures) from dark orange paper; shade around edges with brown and orange chalks. Layer one circle over two side-by-side circles. Punch ivy leaf (Emagination Crafts) from two colors of green paper; detail with green chalks. Freehand cut stem from tan paper; add curled wire tendrils to complete.

APPLE BASKET Punch small apples (EK Success) from yellow, red and green papers. Snip stems from green apples with scissors; mount to back of yellow and red apples. Give dimension to fruit with green and yellow chalks. Follow the illustration below to "weave" apple basket. Cut a 1¾ x 2" rectangle from brown paper. Slice strips into rectangle at ¼" intervals, making sure not to cut all the way to bottom of rectangle. Slice five ¼ x 3½" strips to "weave" basket. Begin weaving strips into sliced rectangle with under/over technique. Glue ends down and trim into basket shape. Slice a ½ x 2" strip for top of basket. Pierce two small holes at center of strip; string cotton thread through holes for basket handle.

SUNFLOWER Punch two jumbo suns (Marvy/Uchida) from two shades of yellow paper. Shade with brown chalk before mounting atop one another. Punch medium circle (Marvy/Uchida) from brown paper; add highlight with white opaque pen. Punch birch leaves (Family Treasures) from dark green paper. Dry emboss leaf details with stylus. Cut wide strip from tan paper; tear into squares and detail with brown chalk at torn edges.

Mount pumpkin, apple basket and sunflowers on torn squares with self-adhesive foam spacers for dimension. Punch two holes at top and bottom of each torn square; tie with twine to connect each square as shown. Mount and hang from brad on dark green paper strip.

Joan Gosling

Brushing to soften edges

Create a sweet look for baby pages by adding soft chalk details to punched shapes. Slice two border strips from navy blue paper; double mat and mount horizontally over brown paper. Cut title letters from template (Scrap Pagerz). Add pen stroke outline; brush brown chalk along pen outline. Double mat photos; layer blue paper strip over top of photo and first matting. Punch jumbo and small stars (Family Treasures) from yellow paper. Add pen stroke outline; brush with brown chalk along pen outline to soften edges. Punch two small holes in center of large stars and on sides of upper border; tie with twine. Mount stars on border and top of photos as shown.

Alison Beachem

Make Your Mark With Pens & Pencils

FRIENDS

Friendship is Special! Deanna and Valerie, Saren and Jaden

Ready, Set, GOOOO!!
Uncle Dick looks ready to charge the camera.

Enjoy the exhilarating colors of pens and pencils. The incredible selection and variety of these colorants allow you to create an ensemble of artistic effects.

Outline shapes and add details with a black, fine-point journaling pen. Make highlights with a white gel pen. Use brush pens for loud intense colors. Cast shadows with a watermark pen. Blend or pull color with a blender pen. Splatter ink from a pen with a spray bulb.

For a sketched effect, use colored pencils and apply pencil strokes in one consistent direction. To create a shadow, apply color to the left side of the shape then reduce the pressure as you move to the right. Experiment with watercolor pencils for a painterly effect. A stroke of a wet brush will turn a solid line into a fluid wash.

The designs and details you can make with this medium will entice you to take out your pens and pencils. Turn the pages to learn how to miraculously turn a flower shape into a decadent hibiscus, a shell shape into an ocean treasure and a few oval shapes into a bouquet of red roses.

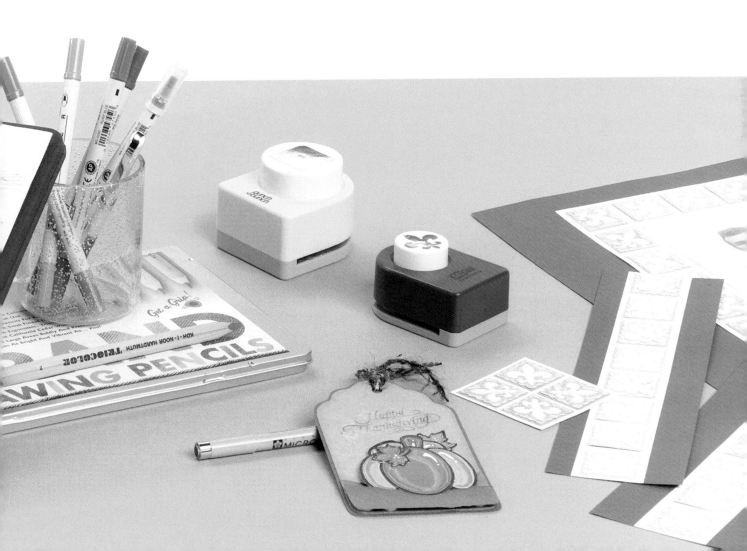

Using contrasting colors for shape definition

Detail punched flowers with contrasting pen colors: black to outline shape and white to highlight it. Quadruple mat photo on solid and patterned (Colors By Design) papers. Layer over solid-colored matted background. Cut title letters from template (source unknown); outline with black fine-point pen. Follow the punch progression steps below to create flower clusters: Punch mega circle (Emagination Crafts) from purple patterned paper; snip small "v's" at edge of circle as shown. Outline shape with fine-tip black pen. Highlight flowers with white opaque gel pen. Punch same size circle from green paper for leaves; trim into oval shape as shown. Detail with black and white pens. Punch medium flower (Punch Bunch) from white paper and ½" circle from yellow paper. Outline both with black pen; detail flower's center with pink opaque pen. Create small white flowers (EK Success) in the same manner. Layer on large flower as shown. Punch large tulip (Nankong) from yellow paper; snip bulb from stem and leaves. Craft small leaves the same way as large leaves using a small circle punch. Outline tulip bulb and leaves with black pen; highlight with pink and white opaque pens. Layer flowers on page as shown; complete with journaling using white opaque gel pen.

Alison Beachem; Photo Donna Morgan

Creating depth and detail

Accent punched shapes with pen stroke outlines and shaded details. Punch small flower (EK Success) from purple patterned paper and leaves (EK Success) from green paper. Punch ¼" circles from yellow paper for center of flowers. Punch jumbo flowerpot (Emagination Crafts) from brown paper. Add pen stroke outlines to all shapes. Complete details by shading with a watermark pen (Tsukineko) before assembling on card as shown.

Alison Beachem

Accenting a photo mat

Fashion a festive floral border from a variety of punched shapes. Punch medium circles (Family Treasures) from blue and green papers; snip "v's" into edge of blue circles to create flowers. (See punch progression steps on previous page.) Cut leaves from green circles. Punch small and medium stars (Family Treasures) from purple and orange papers. Punch small flower (EK Success) from purple paper and ¼" circles (Fiskars) in all colors for center of flowers. Layer all punched shapes atop one another as shown; mount together. Outline all shapes with black fine-point pen.

Alison Beachem

Outlining with whimsical pen strokes

Add a touch of lightheartedness with simple pen and marker strokes—a technique that works well with any punched shape—whenever a little dimension without added bulk is desired. Note how the two shades of ink create depth in the design. Mat photo, embellish with pens and adhere. Freehand draw title and journaling block; shade and outline with pens and adhere. Follow the punch progression steps to create border and corner design: Punch several jumbo birch leaves and flowers (Family Treasures) from white and light green cardstock. Start with a complementary-colored brush marker to trace an outline around shapes, adding swirls and curls on flower centers as desired. Trace over the first line with a black journaling pen. Add yellow punched ½" circle to flower centers, color with brush and black journaling pen to complete.

Pam Klassen, Photo Tina Heine

Variations

As you can see, this is an easy coloring technique that lends a trendy look to any punched shape. For these roses, freehand cut stems from green paper; assemble and adhere. Punch jumbo eggs (Nankong) from pink and red papers. Trace outlines first with complementary-colored brush markers, then again with a black journaling pen to form rose buds. Repeat with jumbo birch leaves (Family Treasures), punched from green paper. Assemble "rose buds" and adhere atop stems. Tuck leaves beneath stems to complete.

Pam Klassen

Variations

Try this with bright, primary-colored papers or softer, pastel shades of paper. Regardless of your paper color, follow this rule of thumb: For best results, use a brush marker that is one shade darker than your paper and a journaling pen that is two shades darker than your paper (or black). Jumbo leaf, heart, flower, star (all Family Treasures); shell (Nankong); sailboat (Emagination Crafts).

Pam Klassen

Drawing subtle shadows

Layered punched shapes are given subtle definition when details are drawn with a watermark pen. Watermark pen strokes don't change the color of the paper; they simply tone it a shade darker, perfect for adding definition or creating shadows. Slice a 2" wide strip of dark green paper for border background. Slice a ¾" strip of mauve paper, a 1⅛" strip of burgundy paper, and ⅜" and ¼" strips of light green paper. Layer all strips over dark green background as shown. Use VersaMark® watermark pen (Tsukineko) to draw a line down each side of mauve and burgundy strips to give a hint of definition. Punch 1" and 1⅛" decorative squares from light and dark blue papers. Punch medium flower (Family Treasures) from dark blue paper and hearts for smaller flower with three-heart corner punch (Fiskars) from light blue paper. Assemble four hearts together to resemble a flower; layer over dark blue flower and layered decorative squares. Complete design with burgundy ¼" punched circles. Detail light blue decorative square with watermark pen and blue fine-point pen. Add pen strokes to hearts with blue brush pen. Mount layered design on border as shown, alternating with punched ½" triangles outlined with watermark pen.

Karen Lewis

Detailing shapes

Piece together an elegant bloom from shaded and detailed punched and freehand drawn shapes. Follow the punch progression steps below to craft the petals, sepals and leaves. Punch large birch leaf (McGill) from mauve and blue paper for petals; trace around edges with watermark pen. Trace along watermark line with black fine-point pen; add dotting and inside-petal details. Trace over inside-petal details with watermark pen to complete. Craft sepals by slicing a segment from a large tooth punch (Emagination Crafts) in green paper as shown. Freehand draw stem and leaves. Draw watermark border on the right side of leaves; add leaf veins with black fine-point pen. Lightly brush black chalk along main vein line. Assemble flower starting with the stem and leaves, and working up to the petals and sepals.

Karen Lewis

Creating dimensional flowers

A dimensional display of flowers with pen and chalk accents highlight a hand-stitched border. Follow the punch progression steps below to create the flowers. WILD THISTLE Punch two medium oak leaves (Family Treasures) from plum paper and one small egg (Carl) from green paper. Slice small segment from wide part of egg; layer over oak leaves. Draw crosshatch design on snipped egg and mount over punched stem with leaves (Family Treasures). TULIP Punch two small raindrops (EK Success) from pink paper and stem with leaves (Family Treasures) from green paper. Layer one raindrop atop another to resemble bulb; shade one side of shapes with pink chalk. Snip all but lower leaves on stem; shade with green chalk. BLACK-EYED SUSAN Punch large daisy (Carl) from golden yellow paper. Cut in half and layer both sides atop one another. Punch ⁵⁄₁₆" circle from dark brown paper; snip off small segment as shown. Detail with black fine-tip pen at center of flower and brown chalk on petals. Layer over punched stem with leaves. DELPHINIUM Punch small flowers with five-flower corner punch (McGill) from blue paper. Follow step 1 below to give three-dimensional quality to small flowers. Mount flowers over small self-adhesive foam spacers as shown below; layer over punched stem with leaves (Family Treasures). Add chalk details to leaves. Follow step 2 below to stitch punched 2⅛" squares (Marvy/Uchida); mount one flower on each square and journal botanical name with black pen.

Valerie Brincheck

1 Place small punched flowers on a mouse pad. Push a black fine-tip pen into the center of each flower to simultaneously accent the center and curl the petals.

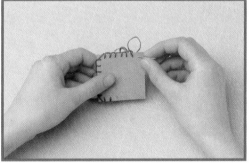

2 Punch holes with a ¹⁄₁₆" circle one-quarter inch from edge of square at quarter-inch intervals. Use a sewing needle and embroidery thread to create a blanket stitch (see diagram) around the outer edges of punched square.

BLANKET STITCH Push needle up through the back at A and down at B, leaving some slack. Come up at C, inside the A/B loop, and pull slack tight. Push needle down at D and up through E, inside the C/D loop. Repeat for desired design.

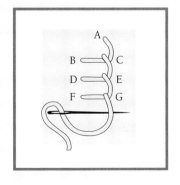

Combining shading techniques

An artistic rendering of a pussy willow combines clever shading on punched shapes with a touch of illustration. Punch small ovals (Family Treasures) and eggs (Family Treasures) from white paper. Follow the progression steps below to shade punched shapes: Shade with gray marker at center and bottom of shape to give illusion of roundness. Dot over gray area, trailing dots a little into the white area with brown fine-tip pen. Concentrate dots at heaviest part of gray shading. Use a yellow brush pen to outline around edge of shape, making sure to leave some white space around gray shading. Freehand draw branches with brown brush tip marker. Punch water drops and crescents (both Fiskars); layer on drawn branches to resemble knots. Color punched shapes with brown marker to complete.

Pennie Stutzman

"I feel wonderfully free from some of the tedious assembly that is synonymous with punch art."

-Pennie Stutzman

Giving shapes washed color and shine

Colored pens and pencils detail seaside shapes resting upon a pen-splattered background. Create the splattered background with a marker attached to a spray bulb (EK Success). Squeeze bulb over white paper to give desired effect. Hold pen close to paper for dense dotting and intense color; pull away for scattered dotting and subtle color. Repeat with a variety of colors. Slice a 2" strip of pen-splattered paper for border; double mat. Punch shells, starfish (both Emagination Crafts) and angelfish (HyGlo/AmericanPin) from tan paper. Follow the progression steps below to detail and glaze shapes: Draw designs on shells and fish with watercolor pencils (Staedtler). See step 1 to "wash" and blend colored pencil designs. Apply paper glaze (Duncan) over shapes. Let dry completely before mounting on border strip.

Nick Nyffeler

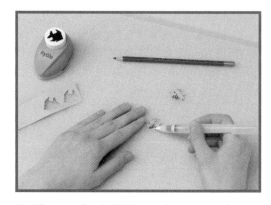

1 Fill a water brush (EK Success) reservoir with water. Lightly trace over watercolor pencil strokes with water brush to achieve a painterly effect. Let dry completely before applying paper glaze.

Brushing watercolor details

Vivid water-colored hibiscus flowers reflect the colorful tone of a Polynesian-themed page. Punch large flower (Nankong) from ivory paper. Follow the progression steps below to give colorful dimension to flowers: Brush light watercolor shade around edges and at center of flower. Select a second, more intense color, and repeat at the middle of the flower. Repeat the above steps two more times, selecting a more intense, vivid color with each step. Blend colors between each step with a water brush. Mat speckle-stamped (Close To My Heart) paper over brown cardstock. Double mat photo and journaling block with black and orange and purple, color-blocked matting. Print journaling on vellum; cut to size and layer over flower. Adhere title sticker letters (Stickopotamus) onto plum paper; silhouette words. Reduce postcard memorabilia on color copier; cut to size and mount on page. Mount punched flowers at corners with self-adhesive foam spacers over green paper yarn (Making Memories) border.

Nick Nyffeler and Janetta Wieneke

Mimicking "pointillism"

Detailed pencil strokes and dots create the postimpressionist look of 19th-century French artist Seaurat. Punch 1¼" squares (Family Treasures) from gray paper and decorative squares (Family Treasures) and fleurs-de-lis (McGill) from ivory paper. See progression steps below to detail decorative square: Begin by drawing thin lines with penciled up and down strokes and then with left to right strokes creating a crosshatch design. Next, draw diagonal lines in one direction. Mount fleur-de-lis on decorative square; detail with short, quick pencil strokes along edges and at interior of fleur-de-lis. Shade around fleur-de-lis on decorative square to give shadow effect. Mount completed pencil work on gray square; mount all squares around 7½ x 9" photo mat as shown. Print title on ivory paper; cut to size and mount.

Jenna Beegle

Charles Auguste Rochefoucault - April 1887

"If you never play, you'll never learn."

-Jenna Beegle

Experimenting with pencil-shading techniques

There are a variety of ways to create shadows and definition by simply changing the direction, intensity and style of pencil strokes used. Lines, dots, zigzags—even small "x's"—when grouped together, can give definition to a flat object. Follow the progression steps at right to shade the punched fleur-de-lis designs. Vary pencil strokes in one direction—up and down, side to side or diagonally. Use a fine or heavy lead pencil to dot a dense background. Vary the density of dotting depending on the amount of definition desired. Experiment with pencil strokes to reflect the tone of your page.

Jenna Beegle

Casting light on a pattern

Mimic the direction of a light source and give dimension to a punched pattern—this one is similar to a pattern in the *Armada* portrait of Elizabeth I—by blending watercolor pencils with a damp paintbrush. Begin with a dark background. Punch medium teardrops (Emagination Crafts), small flowers (All Night Media) and ⁵⁄₁₆" circles from light-colored cardstock. Adhere punched elements to background in desired pattern, using a ruler to help form straight lines. Add title, nameplate and matted photo. Follow the step below to "cast light" across the pattern.

Jenna Beegle

1 Use a black watercolor pencil to draw lines on design to mimic where shadows would fall based on the direction of an imagined or implied light source. Study the art shown to help you get a feel for this concept, or hold an object in front of a sunny window to see how shadows are cast based on an actual light source. Then brush a damp paintbrush across pencil strokes to create a charcoal-like shading effect.

Daubing shapes for realistic definition

Assemble a colorful harvest swag detailed with realistic ink shading. The best tool to use to shade with inks is a dauber, which is a small tool with a sponge tip. Press dauber on inkpad and then lightly dab on area to be shaded; vary intensity of shading and color by adjusting the amount of pressure applied with the dauber. For the design shown here, detail all punched shapes before mounting on page. Make sure to ink all highlights and shadows on the same side of each punched piece so that the light source appears to be shining from one direction. Follow the progression steps to assemble and detail the swag. Let all shapes dry for a few hours before drawing extra highlights with white opaque gel pen. Mount on page as shown over double-matted photo punched with corner designs (Emagination Crafts). Begin layering bouquet with freehand cut wheat stalks, apples and wheat heads. Complete with freehand drawn pen lines extending out from wheat heads with brown pen. Computer print title/journaling on white paper; cut to size and double mat.

Valerie Brincheck

WHEAT Punch 21 mini teardrops (Fiskars): 15 from golden yellow paper and 6 from soft yellow paper. Punch medium rectangle (Family Treasures) from golden yellow paper. Layer golden yellow teardrops up both side of rectangle as shown. Layer soft yellow teardrops up the middle; use mini dauber with brown pigment ink to shade outside tips of teardrops.

GRAPES Punch ⁵⁄₁₆" circles (McGill) from two shades of purple paper for grapes. Using a small, mini dauber and white inkpad, highlight one side of each circle with light quick dabs. Punch large and small grape leaves (Emagination Crafts) from green paper; highlight one side with white ink and shade the other side with eggplant-colored ink.

APPLES Punch medium apples (Carl) from red paper and small birch leaves (Marvy/Uchida) to layer behind apples. Give highlights and shadows to shapes with white and coordinating colors of ink.

Ready, Set, GOOOO!!
Uncle Dick looks ready to charge the camera.

"Nothing in life is one flat color so why should punch art be that way? Also, keep in mind a light source when shading; it will look more realistic."

-*Valerie Brincheck*

Adding artistic effects

A colorful fruit and vine border is given dimension with pen strokes, chalking and self-adhesive foam spacers. Follow the progression steps below for shading techniques: Punch medium apples (Family Treasures) from red paper; draw lines at the top and bottom with red pen. Draw shorter lines over red ones with brown pen. Lightly brush brown and black chalk around edges; complete with white gel pen highlights and brown pen details on the stem. Punch leaves (Emagination Crafts) from green paper; outline leaf with thick green pen. Add veins at middle of leaf with fine-tip green pen, and then again with a fine-tip brown pen. Lightly brush green and brown chalk around edges of leaf to complete. Punch ½" and ¼" circles (EK Success) from light orange and dark purple papers respectively. Shade oranges on one side with dark orange chalk; add navel with brown fine-tip pen and highlight with white opaque gel pen. Shade grapes with black chalk at center and then highlight with white opaque gel pen. Freehand draw and cut vine; shade with pen and chalk similar to leaves. Layer vine on matted border strip; mount fruits and leaves over vine as shown. Mount oranges with small self-adhesive foam spacers for extra dimension. Slice extra thin pieces of brown paper with craft knife; curl by wrapping around a pencil. Layer on border as shown.

Alison Beachem

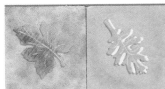

Adding highlights to distress art

Rubbing the punch art and its background with blends of chalk add timeworn appeal. Punch and adhere alternating colors of mega squares (Nankong) along on a 1¾" paper border strip. Accent squares with jumbo and large punched white oak, dusty miller and grape leaves (all Emagination Crafts); fern (Punch Bunch), birch leaf (Nankong) and small acorns (EK Success). Rub brown and orange chalks atop squares and punch art to age. Add white gel pen details (Staedtler).

Alexandra Bleicher

Blending for artistic flair

Exquisitely detailed flowers are shaded with pastel pencils before assembling as a photo frame. Pastel pencils are easy to control and work great for detailing small spaces. After shading with pencils, blend with a blender pen or blending stump (found at art supply stores) to soften strokes. Pastel pencil colors can be applied lightly at first and then intensified with subsequent applications. Follow the progression steps on the next page to layer and detail flowers and leaves. Mount quadruple matted photo over background of patterned vellum (K & Company) on solid paper. Print journaling on vellum; cut to size, back with colored paper and mat. Attach eyelets before mounting on page. Layer flowers and leaves around matted photo as shown.

Nancy Hamby

Anna Faye Smith
Beloved Mother, Grandmother & Friend
February 4, 1932 – October 22, 2002
"You taught us about faith, love & family"

DAISY Punch jumbo daisy (Nankong) from mauve and pink papers. Shade mauve flower first; draw at inside of petals with burgundy pencil. Blend well with smooth strokes away from center of flower and add pen lines at outside of petals with black fine-tip pen. Next, shade pink daisy at inside of petals; blend and add black pen strokes from inside of petal out toward edges. Complete with pen strokes and dotting at outside of petals with white opaque gel pen. Punch ½" circle from yellow paper for center of flower. Color on one side of circle with burgundy pencil; blend well before dotting with black and white pens along shaded area before layering on flower.

FIVE-PETAL FLOWER Punch flower (Nankong) from lavender and purple papers. Shade purple flower first at petal curves with purple pencil and blend. Draw along blended area with fine-tip black pen. Next, shade lavender flower at inner area of petal with purple pencil; blend well toward outside of petals before adding black pen strokes over shading. Complete petals with pen strokes around edges and dotting over blended area with white opaque pen. Punch ½" circle from yellow paper for center of flower. Shade in the same manner as daisy, but use purple ink.

"Textured paper will cause your colors to be rougher when you try to blend them. For a smooth blend, use smooth paper and practice!"

-Nancy Hamby

SIX-PETAL FLOWER Punch flower (Nankong) from two shades of light blue paper. Shade the darker flower first at the outside edges of each petal. Blend well before adding dots over shaded area with black fine-tip pen. Next, shade lighter flower at center and edges of petal; blend well. Draw pen strokes from inside of petals toward the outside over shaded area with black fine-tip pen. Complete with black and white dotting at edges of black pen strokes. Punch circle for center of flower; detail with blue pencil in same fashion as other two flowers before layering. Punch leaves (Nankong) from light and dark green papers. Shade with bright and dark green pencils; blend well before adding black and white curved pen strokes down center of leaves.

Enhancing re-punched shapes

Give punched flowers unique details by re-punching and layering vibrantly colored petals. Use three shades of colored pencils to create colored flowers. Shade the inner third of the petal with the darkest color, moving to the center third with the next lightest color. Color outer third of petal with the lightest pencil. Blend all colors together by lightly shading over all three colors with darkest pencil. Follow the punch progression steps below to color and detail flowers. Mat photo; layer over matted patterned vellum (source unknown). Mount leaves and flowers on page as shown with self-adhesive foam spacers.

JoAnn Colledge

DAISIES Punch daisies (Nankong) from white paper and pink and purple vellum. Shade inner third of petal area on white flower with purple pencil; color next two segments with lighter colors and blend. Punch teardrop (Fiskars) shape at inner edge of each petal. Punch three ⅛" circles into center of flower. Punch small circle from yellow vellum. Layer vellum circle at center of flower; layer colored flower over pink and purple vellum to complete. Snip off four petals for half flowers. Punch leaves (Nankong) from vellum; detail with colored pencils in two shades of green.

Shading layered shapes

Layers of heavily shaded ovals are pieced together to form a bold pumpkin. Follow the progression steps below to assemble and shade pumpkin. Punch five ovals (Marvy/Uchida); mount each one on black paper and silhouette trim leaving a thin border. Layer and adhere together. Repeat steps with maple leaf (Marvy/Uchida) punch and freehand cut stem. Color with dark orange, medium orange and bright yellow colored pencils to shade along the ovals' curves. Start with the darkest color at the outside and move inward using the lighter colors. For the leaves, use a bright green and bright yellow pencil to shade inner area of leaf, making sure to not color all the way to the edge of shape. Blend and mute colors by lightly coloring over shaded area with a white colored pencil. Outline shapes with black fine-tip pen. Add white highlights with a white opaque gel pen; outline area with black fine-tip pen. Cut tag using template (Provo Craft); shade around edges with brown chalk. Tear two brown paper strips, one wider than the other. Mount one strip as background on the tag and the other with self-adhesive foam spacers as the foreground. Mount pumpkin with self-adhesive foam spacers tucking the bottom of it behind foreground torn paper strip. Mat tag on black paper and silhouette cut. Punch hole at top; tie with fibers (EK Success). Adhere seasonal sentiment sticker (Mrs. Grossman's).

Sue Sherman

> ## "A few colored pencils and you've greatly expanded the possibilities of whatever punches you have on hand."
>
> -Sue Sherman

Adding highlights

A dangling apple happily hangs in a round re-punched frame enhanced with pen details. See the step shots below to create the round frame and re-punched shapes. Attach eyelet at top of circle frame and apple. Connect the two with curled and twisted wire. Accent apple, leaf and frame with black and white opaque pen strokes as shown.

Sue Sherman

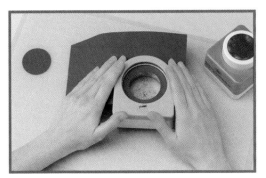

1 Punch jumbo circle into blue cardstock; set the punched circle aside. Flip mega circle punch over, insert and center first negative circle and re-punch to form frame.

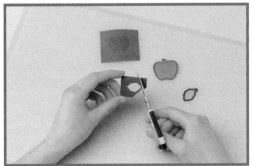

2 Punch and then re-punch leaf and apple in the same manner as step 1. Back the apple with red vellum and the leaf with green vellum, trimming off any overlap.

Make a Splash With Paint

SPECIAL

TREASURES

My chest of drawers made from discarded fruit crate boxes. This is one of my favorite finds while out antique shopping with my Best Friend Becca. I use it in my home studio to hold my ever-growing collection of rubber stamps.

December 2002

Experience the spontaneity of painting. Give up some control and let the paintbrush work for you. You will be surprised with what you can convey with this dynamic medium.

Make your own background paper with household items and a palette of paint. Use a loofah sponge, bunched up plastic wrap or bubble wrap to make intriguing textures. Carve into paint with fork tines. Lift out color with a dry cotton ball. Reapply paint to build up intensity. Make gradations in hue using a wide brush. Create texture using a firm stippling brush. Flatten out paper after it dries by placing it under a heavy book.

Experiment with watercolor paints to create a wet wash. Brush on pearl pigment powder, either wet or dry, for an iridescent effect. Try pearl paints for a luminous look. Choose among a spectrum of radiant colors.

Practice painting and discover how to create movement on paper. In this chapter, find out how to use paint and your punches to create dazzling dragon flies; shimmering rainbow trout; majestic, snowy evergreens and more.

Adding texture with painted backgrounds

Create textured backgrounds for punched and stamped sentiments with a variety of objects found around the house. Everyday items such as plastic wrap, a toothbrush, plastic fork or even a loofah sponge can be used to press into wet ink and create an interesting background design. See the step shots on the following page to achieve a variety of interesting background designs. Stamp sentiment (Serendipity Stamps) with black ink at center of heart. Mat the photo, printed title and journaling. Layer hearts at sides of page. Using a piercing tool or sewing needle, pierce small holes in hearts and photo mat completely through the page; stitch with thin thread to connect hearts to photo mat.

Julie Mullison

1 Apply opaque paint (ChartPak) directly to block stamp (Hero Arts); draw lines through wet paint using a piercing tool, sewing needle or even a plastic fork. Stamp "painted" image onto paper; let dry completely before punching with mega heart punch (Family Treasures).

2 Apply opaque paint directly to block stamp. Blot with a cotton ball to remove sections of wet paint from random areas of the stamp's surface. Stamp "painted" image onto paper; let dry before punching with mega heart punch.

"Keep in mind to play, play, play. You may even end up doing something by mistake that you truly love."

-Julie Mullison

3 Apply different colors of opaque paint directly to block stamp using your fingertips to blend and swirl wet colors together. Stamp "painted" image onto paper; let dry before punching with mega heart punch.

Adding sizzle to embossed-paper shapes

Bring punch art to life in vivid color by brushing some splashes of water-drenched pigment powder to embossed paper designs before punching. Begin with a 12 x 12" burgundy background layered with a sheet of 8½ x 11" patterned paper (Club Scrap) mounted to left side of page. Mount photo with photo corners (Canson) in center of page. Add title (ARTchix Studio) and journaling block to right side of page. Follow the steps on the next page to color the punch art. Mat painted art with 2⅞" wavy square (Family Treasures) punched cardstock and adhere to page to finish.

Erikia Ghumm

1 Use an old CD-ROM for a palette. Dip brush in water, then in Perfect Pearls pigment powder (Ranger). Mix together on CD until the consistency of water paint. Paint embossed designs in true-to-life colors; let dry.

2 Use lighter and darker shades of Perfect Pearls to add highlights and lowlights to embossed design; let dry.

"I keep all the pieces I have practiced on and use them in other art projects like card making and collage. Nothing is wasted when you have learned a new technique."

-Erikia Ghumm

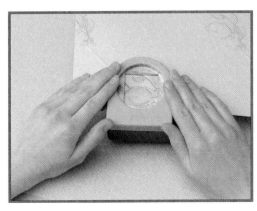

3 Turn a jumbo square punch (Emagination Crafts) upside down; insert painted design, center design and punch. Repeat as needed to create the number of painted squares desired.

Add simple elegance to intricate shapes

With a couple quick strokes of a paintbrush, you can easily add a touch of class to any punched shape. These Asian-inspired punches come alive with a simple, painted border of Perfect Pearls (Ranger). Cut a strip of patterned paper (Magenta) for a background border. Punch Asian house, good luck symbol and dragon (All Night Media) into red and magenta papers. Turn a jumbo square punch (Family Treasures) over, insert and center house and symbol designs one at a time and repunch. Insert dragon, center and lower the design so when it is punched the dragon is at the lower edge of the square punch.

Erikia Ghumm

Simulating a snowy scene with stippling

Realistic details of a snowy landscape are achieved by layering punched trees amongst a soft stippled background. Begin by tearing two strips of paper; one in forest green, the other in dark green. Layer strips over sage green background, with the darkest color in the foreground. Punch tree pairs (McGill) from the two lighter shades of paper. Punch jumbo trees (Nankong) from darkest green paper; set aside. Follow the steps to the right to create stippled background. Mat with white cardstock and add journaled greeting.

MaryJo Regier

"The realism of photos can help you translate depth, distance and lighting perspectives into any punch art coloring technique."

-MaryJo Regier

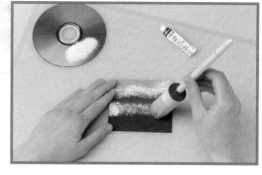

1 Using a stipple brush, softly dab white opaque paint (ChartPak) along tear lines to form low-lying clouds and background.

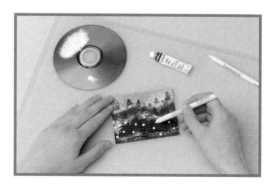

2 Working from background to foreground, mount trees, tucking some behind torn paper edges. Keep in mind visual perspective by mounting lightest colored and smallest trees first in the background, and the larger, darker trees in the foreground. Add extra depth with self-adhesive foams spacers behind a few of the foreground trees. Dab stippling brush over torn edges and trees again to bring clouds atop trees.

3 Use a pointy, foam-tip applicator (Tsukineko) to dab tiny white snowflakes in background of scene and a bullet-tip applicator to dab larger white snowflakes in foreground.

Inking and stamping a faux finish

This magnificent wreath of detailed leaves looks more complicated to create than it is! The leaves get their colors from daubed and stippled ink and a simple stamped design. A large variety of leaf punches are layered to create this full wreath, but you can build one with only three different leaf shapes. Leaves included in this design are: large and small maple, large birch and large and small oak leaves (all McGill); large grape and large and small dusty miller leaves (all Emagination Crafts). Use brightly colored cardstock to keep leaf colors vivid after detailing with brown inks. Punch a number of leaves from orange, yellow, lime, brown and teal cardstocks. Follow the progression steps below to detail leaves: First, stipple or daub ink (see pages 42 and 54 for how-to) on punched leaf with brown or tan ink colors. Next, stamp crackle design (Stampers Anonymous) with sepia or dark brown ink on leaf to resemble leaf veins. After leaves are dry, begin layering wreath at bottom center over photo mounted on double-matted cardstock. Assemble wreath up and around photo, layering leaves with small pieces of self-adhesive foam spacers. Randomly add black iridescent glass beads over leaves with glue. Ink and stamp title block in similar fashion as leaves. Write title with black embossing pen, sprinkle with black embossing powder and set with embossing gun. Double mat and layer over ribbon strips snipped into "v's" at the ends.

Donna Pittard

"Don't have an expectation of what the finished art should look like."

-Donna Pittard

Painting and embossing a delicate design

Upscale watering cans achieve their chic look with a hand-painted and embossed floral design. To begin, punch watering can (Punch Bunch) from green paper. Practice painting with Radiant Pearls paint (Angelwings Enterprises) and thin, "detail" paintbrush on scrap paper to gain confidence. Use smooth, loose brush strokes for best results; paint flowers and stamens first before adding stems and leaves. See step shot below for how to paint design on punched shape. After completing painted design, sprinkle clear embossing powder on wet paint, shake off excess and set with embossing gun. Mount punched shapes on torn mulberry squares, then again on burgundy torn paper squares. Mount squares on green torn paper strip brushed with teal chalk around the edges. Wrap fibers (Fibers by the Yard) between torn squares. Double mat on burgundy (Paper Adventures) and green (Magenta) torn patterned paper strips. Layer at left side of page. Tear thin strips of burgundy and green patterned paper; mount at right side of page as shown. Double and triple mat photos on solid, mulberry and torn paper; mount with red photo corners (Kolo) on matting. Cut title letters using template (Scrap Pagerz); brush edges with teal chalk and layer over mulberry paper scraps. Silhouette-tear mulberry paper around each letter; mount with self-adhesive foam spacers. Punch small flower (EK Success) from green paper; detail with Radiant Pearls paint, set with embossing powder and mount on title. Attach eyelet (Making Memories) and layer on torn mulberry paper scrap. Print journaling on vellum; tear around edges before mounting to page with mini eyelets.

Kari Hansen-Daffin; Photos Tira Scott

1 Use a small, thin "detail" paintbrush to freehand paint floral design with Radiant Pearls paint on punched watering cans. If desired, photocopy onto card-stock floral patterns shown above and then apply paint.

Using watercolors to paint a feminine motif

Paint a colorful, detailed floral motif with watercolors on punched hearts. Mix watercolors with a small amount of water to achieve a thick consistency. Using a fine "detail" brush, practice designs with loose strokes on scrap paper. Punch small (EK Success) and large (Emagination Crafts) primitive hearts from white paper. Paint flower petals and stamens first at upper area of heart as shown below in the paint progression steps. Next, add leaves and small dots. Complete with diagonal brush strokes for lattice. Mount hearts on mulberry paper; silhouette tear around edges. Mount with self-adhesive foam spacers on torn purple pressed paper. Punch two ⅛" holes on both sides of each heart. Weave sheer ribbon (Offray) through holes; tie a knot at each end of ribbon and double mat. Mat photo and journaling block. Mount both over large solid-colored paper detailed with woven ribbon as shown and described above; layer over patterned paper (Karen Foster Design).

Kari Hansen-Daffin, Photo Jodi Amidei

People have often told me that there is a sparkle in your eyes. I have seen it since you were a small toddler. That sparkle is bright and clear in this photo. I think that is why I have always been drawn to this picture. It's so clearly you!

"Practice being loose and flowing, instead of tight and nit-picky, when you paint."

-Kari Hansen-Daffin

Combining colorants for interesting effects

A combination of watercolors and pen work adds unique dimension and visual interest to punched shapes. Follow the progression steps below to detail fish: Punch fish (McGill) from ivory paper. Brush green and brown watercolors on fish as shown. Using a black marker (American Crafts) attached to a spray bulb (EK Success), squeeze bulb to create splattered pen design. Give shine and seal colors by adding glaze (Duncan) atop punched shapes. Layer detailed fish on jumbo punched rectangle (Nankong); shade around edges with black chalk. Double mat on patterned paper (Keeping Memories Alive) and textured netting (Avant Card). Mount with paper-torn rectangles on green border strip. Print title and journaling; layer with enlarged photo on solid-colored background. Silhouette large fish from photo; mount with self-adhesive foam spacers.

Kelli Noto

Using double-loaded paint for colorful effect

Vibrantly water-colored dragonflies carry beautiful details on their wings with an artistic paint technique called "double loading." See step shot and progression steps below to paint dragonflies. Flip dragonfly punch (EK Success) over, insert and center painted image; punch out dragonfly. Mat border strip with solid-colored paper. Wrap entire border strip with thin silver metallic fiber (Kreinik). Mount dragonflies on border strip with small self-adhesive foam spacers. Draw dragonfly trails with silver glitter glue (Duncan); allow to dry before handling.

Nick Nyffeler

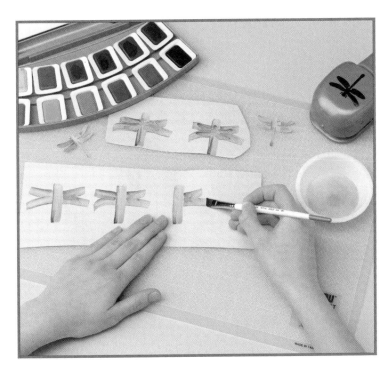

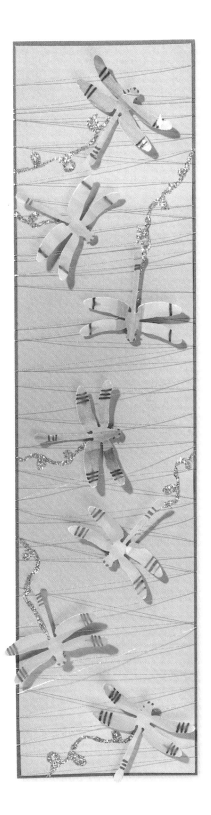

1 Use artistic "double loading" technique to paint water-colored dragonflies. Apply two colors of paint (ChartPak), one to each side of a wide flat paintbrush. Brush one vertical line for dragonfly body. Apply two different colors of paint for dragonfly wings with horizontal strokes. Use small "detail" brush to paint thin vertical stripes on wings and tail. Experiment with double and triple loading different colors of paint for unique color combinations. Apply paper glaze (Duncan) to wing sections only after punching. Allow several hours for glaze to dry before handling dragonflies.

Painting and embossing hand-textured shapes

Piece together a patchwork of stamped and punched shapes detailed with painted "stitching" for an elegant heritage border. Before punching or stamping, give texture to paper by lightly spraying it with water (use a spray bottle with a fine mist). While damp, crumple paper and then iron (set iron to cool setting) to re-flatten. Follow the step shots below to detail and assemble quilt border. Mount border over black background. Quadruple mat photo on crumpled cardstock. Print title; cut to size and double mat. Layer both on ivory paper before mounting on background.

Torrey Miller, Photo Jodi Amidei

Ione Vivian Arndt Hill
with first child, Bruce

1 Punch large squares from a variety of muted colored and textured papers. Stamp flower (All Night Media) and paisley (JudiKins) designs on a few squares using complementary ink colors. Use a metal straightedge ruler and craft knife to diagonally cut a few squares in half. Assemble and adhere triangles and squares into a quilt pattern atop cardstock background; trim away excess background.

2 Punch flowers (Carl, EK Success, McGill) and leaves (Punch Bunch) from solid-colored papers. Mount and adhere shapes on various squares as shown.

3 Use a "detail" paintbrush to apply pearlized gold paint (Angelwings Enterprises) to resemble stitches and outline punched shapes. Paint a small section at a time; sprinkle with clear embossing powder and set with an embossing gun.

Airbrushing vibrant color with ease

Add vibrant gradated color to punched leaves by "airbrushing" with a marker attached to an air canister (both Copic). Punch a variety of leaves (Emagination Crafts, Family Treasures) from white paper. Follow the step shot and progression steps below to "airbrush" leaves. Begin with one color applied to left side of shape; add a second color to complete background. Give highlights and dimension by adding small blasts of darker and lighter colors. Intensity of color will vary depending upon how close the canister is held to paper and how many layers of color are applied. Triple mat photos on solid-colored paper; layer over embossed patterned paper (source unknown). Print title and journaling; cut to size and chalk around edges of journaling block. Layer and mount leaves diagonally on page as shown.

Jodi Amidei; Photos Janetta Wieneke

Wedding Cake

This was the last chance to view this beautiful wedding cake before both Dan and Janetta decided to wear it all over their faces.

1 Insert a marker into an air canister and press canister trigger to "airbrush" color onto punched leaf. Switch marker colors as desired for shading. After airbrushing, add freehand pen stroke veins to leaves to complete coloring.

Variation

Try using found household items—such as taped-together toothpicks, stencils cut from scrap paper, doilies, etc.— for "masks" when applying different layers of color.

Kenneth O'Connell for Copic

Make it Stick With Stamping Inks & Embossing Powders

Tap into the extravagant effects of stamping and embossing. You will find that you can capture almost any mood with this medium. Make your punch art fun and festive, glamorous and glitzy, or elegant and elaborate.

Achieve rich vibrant colors with stamping ink, available in a rainbow of hues. Punch out a stamped image to give it dimension. Stamp your punch art with a watermark ink pad for a subtle change. Brush pearl pigment powder over a watermark image for an iridescent effect.

Experiment with various embossing powders to create majestic relief images. The enticing selection of pearls, tinsels and foils will ignite your imagination. Hold the punched shape with tweezers or a clip pen when applying heat. Be careful not to burn the paper.

Build dimension with thick layers of embossing enamel. For a sculpted touch, try stamping into the final layer of enamel before it cools. Make a lasting impression with stamping and embossing. Read on to master this medium and apply it to your punched shapes to create fluttering butterflies, sparkling holiday lights, dancing Kokopellis and other admirable art.

Brushing pearlized powder for an iridescent glow

This simple technique adds dramatic iridescent color to punched and stamped shapes. Punch mega flower (Emagination Crafts) from black and silver metallic cardstocks. Set silver flowers aside. Follow the step shots on the next page to detail black flowers. Diagonally wrap mauve patterned paper (Provo Craft) with white fibers (EK Success) before matting with solid-colored cardstock. Offset black flowers over silver metallic flowers; layer on page as shown. Mount every third flower with self-adhesive foam spacers for dimension. Die cut title letters (QuicKutz) from silver metallic and black cardstock stamped and colored in similar fashion as flowers; layer on page as shown. Triple mat photo; stamp and color second mat in similar fashion as flowers. Wrap two corners of matted photo with fibers before layering on page over silver metallic rectangle.

Jodi Amidei; Photo Pam Klassen

1 Press Perfect Medium ink pad (Ranger) onto floral stamp (Ye Olde Stamping Grounds); stamp image onto black punched mega flower.

2 Lightly brush Perfect Pearls pigment powders (Ranger) across stamped image. There's no need to heat set images; they will dry on their own.

Stamping ornamental designs

Let the wings of a butterfly carry a rich deco look with a stamped design detailed with pearlized powder and glitter glue dots. Punch jumbo (Family Treasures) and small (McGill) butterflies from black cardstock. Press Versamark watermark ink pad (Tsukineko) onto ornamental stamp (All Night Media); stamp image onto punched butterflies. Lightly brush Perfect Pearls pigment powder (Ranger) across stamped image. Add glitter dots (Suze Weinberg) along edges of wings. Punch jumbo circle (Family Treasures) from black velvet paper and medium oval (Emagination Crafts) from black cardstock. Stamp letters (Hero Arts) for words with watermark ink before brushing with pigment powder. Mount oval over black velvet circle. Mount butterflies and circles on white double matted border strip as shown.

Erikia Ghumm

Enhancing quilt designs with metallic shine

Punched quilt designs take on metallic luster and dimension by embossing with Cloisonné powder (Stampa Rosa). Punch shapes (All Night Media, Emagination Crafts, Punch Bunch) from white paper or from metallic foil for a sharper finish. Follow the step shots below to create metallic designs. Mount on torn paper squares detailed with metallic embossed edges. Begin by tearing paper into a large square. Blot torn edges on a clear embossing pad or color around edges with an embossing pen. Dip torn edges into silver cloisonné embossing powder and carefully heat edges to melt embossing powder. Attach bronze eyelets (Creative Impressions) at top and bottom of each torn paper square; thread with fiber (Funkie Ladiez) to link squares. Mount design on shiny black textured paper adorned with eyelets at corners.

Kim Rudd

1 Punch quilt design (Emagination Crafts) from white cardstock; re-punch with jumbo square (Family Treasures). Gently rub punched design onto embossing pad.

2 Sprinkle moist design with embossing powder; shake off excess.

"Embossing is a very forgiving technique. You can reheat the design several times so it will meld the way you want."

-Kim Rudd

3 Heat with an embossing gun to set the powder. For thicker coverage, repeat steps 2 and 3.

Emphasizing stamped designs with embossing

Embossed designs become visually dramatic shapes when set on black paper. Follow step shot below to create circular designs. Punch kokopellis (Emagination Crafts) from black cardstock. Coat with jewel paint (Delta) for shine and dimension. Layer embossed punched circles and kokopellis at left side of matted brown background as shown. Stamp circle designs on rust-colored cardstock with black ink and emboss to use for photo mat; double and triple mat photos. Punch title letters (EK Success) and layer on teal torn paper strip. Computer print journaling on solid-colored paper; cut to size and mat.

Jodi Amidei

1 Stamp patterned images (Stampers Anonymous) on black paper; sprinkle with colored embossing powders (Ranger) and set with embossing gun. Flip over mega circle punch (EK Success); insert and center stamped image and punch.

Creating texture with embossing powders

A variety of metallic embossing powders take center stage on punched fleur-de-lis shapes. Stamp large leaf design (Stampendous!) on gold metallic paper with embossing ink for background of punched shape. Sprinkle bronze metallic embossing powder on wet image; shake off excess. Set with embossing gun. Punch completed design with jumbo decorative square (Family Treasures). Punch large decorative square (Family Treasures) from black paper; layer over jumbo square. Follow step shot to create metallic fleurs-de-lis.

Valerie Brincheck

1 Create a textured metallic paper to punch fleurs-de-lis from with bronze, gold and silver embossing powders. Begin by applying a clear embossing pad to paper; randomly sprinkle all three embossing powders onto paper. Shake off excess; set with embossing gun. Punch fleur-de-lis shapes (Family Treasures) from textured paper; layer on punched decorative squares.

Embossing a stenciled motif

Utilize a negative punched shape as the perfect stencil for embossing into an eye-catching metallic design. Follow the step shot below to create stenciled design. Layer designs as a border over blue background paper (Magenta.) Attach fiber (EK Success) to right side of page. Layer and mount photos with gold photo corners (Canson) on beige cardstock as shown. Write title with copper accent pen (Ranger) on brown paper; cut to size and mount. Journal with black fine-tip pen. Detail around edges of beige cardstock with glitter glue (Ranger).

Erikia Ghumm, Photos MaryJo Regier

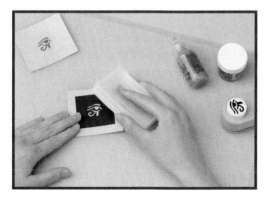

1 Using negative punched shape (All Night Media) as a stencil, stamp through stencil onto tan cardstock with an embossing pad. Lift off stencil; sprinkle stamped image with copper metallic embossing powder (Ranger). Shake off excess powder and set with embossing gun. Flip over jumbo circle punch (Family Treasures), insert and center embossed and negative space image; punch. Detail edges of circle with glitter glue (Ranger).

Showcasing an embossed ensemble

An artistic assembly of circles and moons in calm, cool colors is warmed with gold metallic details. Collect an array of complementary-colored papers to stamp and emboss upon; add texture to teal cardstock (see page 60 for how-to). Follow step shots below to create designs and attach decorative nailheads. Layer completed designs over beige cardstock double-matted with patterned (Emagination Crafts) and solid papers as shown. Layer photo on matted, printed journaling block. Mount over gold metallic paper strip (Canson). Cut title letters from template (Scrap Pagerz) and mount on page.

Torrey Miller, Photo Jodi Amidei

1 Stamp leaf and floral designs (both Stampendous), emboss and heat set (see page 66 for how-to). Insert embossed designs into a flipped-over punch (Family Treasures) and center; punch shape. Insert round punched shapes into round punch again and re-punch to form moon shapes.

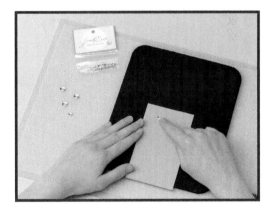

2 To mount spiral nailheads (JewelCraft), push nailhead into front of cardstock with your finger.

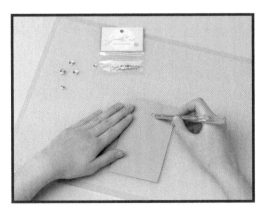

3 Turn cardstock over and use the end of a craft knife to flatten nailhead legs against cardstock.

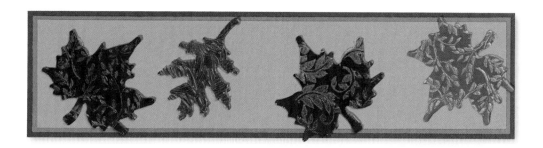

Stamping designs into warm embossing enamel

Glazed leaves adorned with metallic stamped designs are a perfect enhancement on elegant seasonal pages. Punch mega maple and oak leaves (both Punch Bunch) from mustard, berry, green and brown cardstocks. Follow the step shots below to detail leaves. Mount on double matted cardstock border strip.

Julie Mullison

1 Press mega punched leaf onto embossing pad and sprinkle with clear ultra thick embossing enamel (UTEE; Suze Weinberg). Heat leaf from underside with an embossing gun until powder liquifies, then turn over and heat surface. Repeat to thicken coating.

2 While second layer of UTEE is still warm, apply gold dye-based ink to stamp (pigment ink will smear); stamp directly into warm UTEE.

Impressing letters into embossing enamel

Press title letters into twice-layered warm metallic embossing enamel for an interesting "etched" look. Punch maple, hawthorne and grape leaves (all Emagination Crafts) from heavy brown cardstock. Press punched leaf onto an embossing pad and sprinkle with copper ultra thick embossing enamel (UTEE; Ranger). Using tweezers or a clip to hold punched shape, heat from underside with an embossing gun until powder liquifies. Repeat again to thicken layer of UTEE. While second layer is still warm, press in letter stamp (Hero Arts) with black dye-based ink. Mount on double matted border strip with adhesive glue dots. Attach eyelets at corners of border strip; string fiber (source unknown) as a frame through eyelets (Making Memories).

Julie Mullison

Creating faux "hammered tin" accents

Stamp intricate designs into gold metallic ultra thick embossing enamel (UTEE) to create faux "hammered tin" accents. Press embossing pad onto cardstock and sprinkle with gold metallic UTEE (Suze Weinberg). Heat cardstock from underside with an embossing gun until powder liquifies. Add a second layer of UTEE. While UTEE is still warm, press in stamped designs (Magenta, Stampendous, Stampin' Up!). Punch 1" and 2" squares (Emagination Crafts, Family Treasures) out of embossed designs. Mount on sliced border strip as shown over solid-colored background. Cut two 1" squares on the diagonal for photo corners; double mat before mounting on matted photo. Print journaling; cut to size and mount on page.

Torrey Miller,
Photo MaryJo Regier

Our living room is filled with family heirlooms that have been passed down for several generations. Someday, these heirlooms will be passed to my kids, and hopefully will continue down the family lines for years to come.

"Try everything. Sometimes the most amazing effects happen by accident. Remember, there are no mistakes in scrapbooking—only flopportunities!"

-Torrey Miller

Highlighting embossed shapes with rub-ons

Give punched and embossed shapes an "antiqued" look with metallic rub-on details. Punch ornaments, bells and angels (all Emagination Crafts) from colored cardstocks. Follow the steps on the next page to create the ornaments, bells and angels. Add metallic rub-on (Craf-T) highlights and details to cooled shapes with fingertips. Stamp pine tree boughs (Stampin' Up!) with green ink at left side of page as shown. Layer punched shapes over artistic wire "hooks" looped through pierced holes in background paper. Double mat photo with patterned (Creative Imaginations) and solid papers. Print title and journaling; cut to size, mat and mount on page. Layer punched and embossed angels over title block.

Julie Mullison

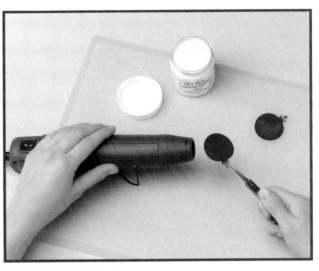

1 Press bulb area of punched shape onto embossing pad; sprinkle with clear UTEE (Suze Weinberg) and set as shown on page 70. Shapes may curl while cooling; to prevent, place slightly warm image under a heavy book, until completely cool. Use your fingertip to apply metallic rub-ons (Craf-T) onto cooled ornaments to "antique" them.

2 Apply a second and third layer of clear UTEE and set with embossing gun to encapsulate color. Add "crackles" by bending shape when cooled, if desired.

Encapsulating color on "antiqued" glass

Re-create a childhood memory with a string of "antiqued" Christmas lights, complete with metallic accents and crackled "glass." Punch large light bulb shape (Emagination Crafts) from colored cardstocks. Follow the step shots above and progression steps to the left to create glass light bulbs. Draw horizontal stripes at base of bulb with embossing pen; sprinkle with gold powder (PSX Design) and set. Layer cooled bulbs over paper yarn (Making Memories) mounted with eyelets (Making Memories) on double matted cardstock strip. Weave green wire (Toner Plastics) under and over bulbs and through eyelets to complete.

Deborah Breedlove

Adding sparkle and shine to shapes

Decorative tags provide the perfect background for punched shapes featured with shimmer and shine. Cut tag from colored cardstock; punch celestial shapes (EK Success, Family Treasures, McGill, Punch Bunch) and mount on tag as shown. Follow the step shot below to detail shapes. Mount eyelet (Impress Rubber Stamps) on tag; tie fibers (Rubba Dub Dub). Mount tags on patterned paper (Paper Adventures). Adhere sticker letters (Colorbök) to solid paper; silhouette cut around words and then over pink metallic tinsel (Magic Scraps) with self-adhesive foam spacers.

Dawn Mabe

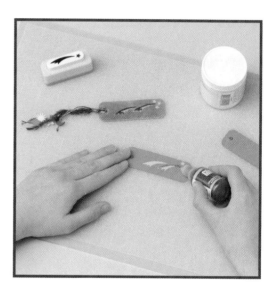

1 Apply glitter glue (Ranger) to edges of galaxy punched shape; allow to completely dry before glazing with a coat or two of clear UTEE to add shine.

Creating bumpy texture with embossing enamel

Playful "moon men" command a presence with their metallic faces and bodies on colorful die-cut tags. Follow step shots below to create "moon men" and decorative shapes. Mount assembled moon men on large die-cut tags (Ellison). Border tag with glitter glue (Ranger); tie sequined fibers (Funkie Ladiez) to tag. Use alphabet stamps (Hero Arts) to stamp words with silver ink onto black cardstock; cut to size and mount on tags. Layer and mount tags with circle/square designs over matted cream background. Mat photos on black cardstock; outline with glitter glue at photos' edges. Adhere title sticker letters (ARTChix Studio) at top of page. Journal with black fine-tip pen.

Erikia Ghumm

1 Stamp face image (Magenta) onto black cardstock with silver ink (Tsukineko). Flip jumbo circle punch (Family Treasures) over, center image and punch. Set faces aside. Flip jumbo square punch (Family Treasures) over; insert negative circle shape and re-punch to form circle/square frame. Apply glitter glue around edges of square.

2 Add iridescent color and texture to cardstock prior to punching. Stamp black cardstock with embossing pad (Ranger); sprinkle with embossing powder (All Night Media). Heat from underside with an embossing gun until powder gets bubbly and let cool.

3 Apply metallic rub-ons (Craf-T) with your fingertip across bubbly surface. Punch doll body (Nankong) and large squares from textured metallic paper. Mat circle/square frame over metallic textured square.

"I like to combine techniques because it adds personal style to my art and takes it to the next level."

-Erikia Ghumm

Make it Magic With Other Coloring Techniques

Explore new ways to enhance your punch art. Don't be limited by the coloring tools and supplies you see in a scrapbook store. The featured artists in this chapter came up with breakthrough and innovative coloring ideas. You can too.

Reinforce a punch's theme by punching through a colorful sticker collage with the same theme. Take an embossing stylus to Scratch-Art® paper and let the underlying colors surprise you. Press tiny beads into embossing enamel for a sparkling emphasis. For an uncommon effect, transfer newsprint or clip art to your punched shapes with an ink-transfer blender pen. Punch images from magazines for a fresh, contemporary look.

Capture the blooming colors of a vibrant pressed flower or practice the art of flower pounding. Simply use a hammer to pound the pigment onto paper, then punch out your desired shape.

Be adventurous and experiment with different tools and techniques. Let your imagination take you to a new place. Discover the undiscovered colorant. Create the unexpected punch art.

Revealing color with Scratch-Art® paper

A childhood favorite that never ceases to amaze the artist—young or old, scratch art is back, easy to do and versatile in its use. Scratching techniques can vary, as can the outcomes. Light strokes back and forth work well on thicker Scratch-Art paper (Scratch-Art Co.), while thinner paper requires scratching in one direction to prevent creasing and/or wrinkling. For a glamorous holiday look, use black Scratch-Art paper with metallic colors hidden underneath. Follow the step shot below to create the detailed shapes shown. Mount designed shapes atop matted punched squares of metallic paper with self-adhesive foam spacers; layer over glossy border strip.

Kelly Angard

1 Punch holiday shapes (Emagination Crafts, Family Treasures, HyGlo/American Pin, Nankong) from Scratch-Art paper; use wooden pointed stylus to scratch designs onto the punched shape.

Scratching designs to uncover a rainbow of colors

White Scratch-Art paper harbors a spectrum of colors underneath just begging to be brought to life. Punch large Star of David (Emagination Crafts), menorah (McGill) and 1¼" squares from white Scratch-Art paper (Scratch-Art Co.) Flip over square punch and align menorah shape at center and re-punch square shape. Use Scratch-Art stylus to detail punched shapes with a variety of designs as shown. Mount detailed shapes on matted border strip as shown. Mat menorah shapes on gold metallic cardstock; mount with self-adhesive foam spacers over metallic ribbon. Punch small dreidles (McGill) from blue cardstock; detail with gold gel pen (Staedtler) before mounting on detailed punched squares with self-adhesive foam spacers. Layer photos on double matted background as shown; mat one photo on white cardstock and the other on white Scratch-Art paper. Scratch zigzag design around edges of matting before mounting on page. Adhere sticker letters (Colorbök) to cut vellum; mount over photo with gold eyelets (Making Memories) at corners. Die cut title letters (Ellison) from dark blue and white Scratch-Art paper. Outline letters and scratch in whimsical design with stylus before layering over blue letters for shadow effect.

Kelly Angard, Photos Kelli Noto

Collaging stickers for colorful backgrounds

A colorful collection of themed stickers from a variety of manufacturers can be collaged on cardstock and used to punch shapes. Layer and adhere Christmas-themed stickers from the following companies: Bo Bunny Press, Colorbök, Karen Foster Design, Mrs. Grossman's, PrintWorks, PSX Design and Stickopotamus. Punch flowers (EK Success) and leaves (Emagination Crafts) from sticker collage as well as cardstock, in shades of red and green. Punch four mittens (Emagination Crafts) from sticker collage. Tear burgundy paper strip; mount over patterned paper (Scrappin' Dreams) as bottom border. Layer solid and collaged punched flowers and leaves; mount some with self-adhesive foam spacers. Mat photos; layer with collaged mittens over paper-torn matting with self-adhesive foam spacers. Mount title letters over matted torn-paper strip. Print journaling on vellum; cut to size and mount on page.

Pam Klassen

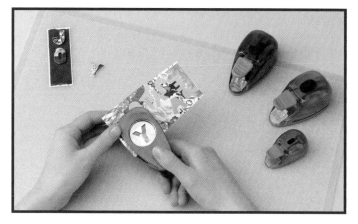

1 Create a sticker collage by applying theme-appropriate stickers randomly to a piece of white cardstock. Punch poinsettia flowers, holly leaf and mittens and title letters from collaged paper. Flip punches over to center and capture sticker designs that you wish to show on your punched shape. If desired, use the leftover collage scraps from which you punch the letters or shapes as additional page design elements.

Layering sticker collage shapes for visual interest

Enhance a collaged page with shapes punched from a sticker-collaged background. Slice two thin strips of purple patterned paper (Faux Memories) before layering with rose-colored paper (Design Originals) for background; mount strips above purple border as shown. Mat portrait on burgundy textured paper (Emagination Crafts). Silhouette cut other photos. Layer and adhere similar-themed stickers (All My Memories, Current, Frances Meyer, The Gifted Line, Mrs. Grossman's, PSX Design, Stampendous, Tie Me To The Moon) on white cardstock. Punch hearts in a variety of sizes and shapes (Emagination Crafts, Family Treasures, Marvy/Uchida). Mat some on textured burgundy paper. Print title and journaling; cut to size. Layer and mount collaged punched hearts, matted photo, silhouette-cropped photos, title and text with self-adhesive foam spacers. Complete page by mounting rhinestone string (Hirschberg Schutz & Co.) around page with glue dot adhesive (Glue Dots International).

Pennie Stutzman

"There is no right or wrong with this technique. You simply place the stickers randomly and the punches frame them magically."

-Pennie Stutzman

Transferring ink from newsprint for contemporary look

Transfer printed matter onto cardstock before punching shapes for a creative twist. Experiment with a variety of image and text sizes to add visually interesting effects to punched shapes. Follow the step shots below to transfer newsprint onto cardstock. Punch jumbo trees (EK Success) from paper in shades of green. Layer torn brown paper with and without transferred text on border strip as shown. "Plant" printed and solid trees along torn paper edges.

Pam Klassen

2 Flip tree punch over; center portion of transferred print that you wish to capture and punch shape. Repeat step 1 on additional cardstock for hills on which to "plant" the trees.

1 Photocopy newspaper, magazine or book print of choice. Place the photocopy face down on cardstock. Rub back of photocopy with ink transfer blender pen (ChartPak); rub again with a bone folder to transfer ink onto cardstock to complete transfer.

Transferring clip art designs onto shapes

Antique maps downloaded from the Internet provide the interesting images on punched boat shapes. Photocopy map clip art; place photocopy face down on white cardstock. Rub back of photocopy with transfer blender pen (ChartPak); rub again with a bone folder to transfer ink onto cardstock. Flip over jumbo boat punch (Emagination Crafts); center portion of transferred print and punch shape. Layer over jumbo (Emagination Crafts) and mega (Punch Bunch) punched squares from marine blue and black cardstock along with small photos with self-adhesive foam spacers. Mat the large photo on blue cardstock before mounting onto light blue background. Journal quote on vellum with black calligraphy pen; cut to size and mount on large photo. Die cut letters (QuicKutz) from blue cardstock and mount on transferred image rectangle; mat on black cardstock with self-adhesive foam spacers.

Kelli Noto

Rubbing on rich details with metallic leaf

Add lustrous effects to punched shapes with metallic leaf details. Punch large sun (EK Success) from black cardstock. Follow the step shots below to detail punched shapes with gold metallic leafing. Complete sun design with copper glitter glue (Duncan) dots around edges. Mat photos on patterned paper (Scrap Ease) before layering on tan background. Mount detailed suns around photos as shown. Cut title letters from textured metallic paper (Emagination Crafts).

Pamela Frye

1 Use a liquid Zig glue pen (EK Success) to freehand draw a spiral at the center of punched sun shape (EK Success). Allow glue to dry until it is tacky to the touch and color is clear.

2 Apply metallic leaf (Biblical Impressions) atop tacky glue spiral by pressing metallic leaf with your fingertips.

3 Use a small, stiff brush to remove excess metallic leaf and reveal your drawn design.

Embellishing enameled shapes with detail

No two snowflakes are identical, as demonstrated here with a variety of snowflakes in different colors and sizes, and with different dimensional embellishments! Punch medium and jumbo snowflakes (Nankong, Punch Bunch) from vellum, silver metallic paper (Lasting Impressions), and white and blue cardstocks. Follow the step shots below to detail snowflakes. Layer completed snowflakes on dark blue speckled cardstock (Paper Garden); mount some with self-adhesive foam spacers. Double mat with white and blue cardstock; tear edges of white matting.

Julie Mullison

1 See page 70 for how to apply and heat clear UTEE. Apply three layers for extra thickness. While third layer is still warm, sprinkle small seed beads (Mill Hill) into enamel and press lightly with fingertips.

2 Apply two layers of clear UTEE. While second layer is still warm, use tweezers to press tiny flecks of metal flakes (Biblical Impressions) into surface. Apply one more layer of clear UTEE to seal.

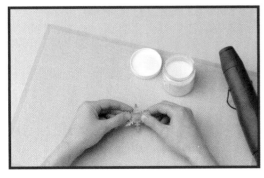

3 Apply three layers of clear UTEE. Once UTEE has cooled, gently bend or curl the enamel-covered snowflake to "crack" the surface.

Layering magazine graphics with punched shapes

A cluster of graphic-embellished roses adorns a torn latticed background. Experiment with the layering and collaging of colorful images that capture your interest from magazines or photos. Here, an assembly of roses in contrasting colors provides a visually interesting border design. Silhouette crop rose images from magazines (treat with de-acidifying spray); set aside. Punch daisy shapes (EK Success) from other rose images; layer over silhouette cut roses. Follow step shot below to mount eyelets (Creative Impressions, Making Memories) at center of images. Tear ½" strips of mauve paper; layer diagonally in both directions on lavender background paper to create lattice. Mount colorful fibers (Quilters' Resource) over torn paper strips. Mount completed flower designs on lattice background with self-adhesive foam spacers. Mat photo on mauve cardstock; tear edges. Print title and journaling onto vellum; mount under fibers with micro eyelets (Making Memories).

Kari Hansen-Daffin

1 To add eyelet, punch a ¼" hole. Insert eyelet; flip eyelet and paper over. Place pointed end of setter into protruding end of eyelet. Tap setter with hammer; remove setter.

Embellishing negative space with glass marbles

Silhouette cut images can provide an excellent canvas for embellishing the negative space of punched designs. Select colorful images from photos or magazines (treated with de-acidifying spray) to use as a background for punched shapes. Silhouette cut image; punch flower (EK Success) into center of image to create negative space. Follow the steps below to embellish the negative space. Mount flowers on card as a border with self-adhesive foam spacers. Double mat photo using torn mulberry paper for second mat. Layer over pink paper and torn patterned paper (Making Memories) strip. Wrap fibers (EK Success) over background paper and card to complete.

Kari Hansen-Daffin

1 Adhere strong, double-sided Wondertape™ (Suze Weinberg) to the back of each negative punched image, completely covering the punched opening.

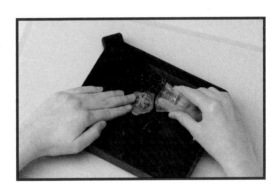

2 Pour tiny glass marbles (Halcraft) onto front of exposed Wondertape and shake off the excess marbles.

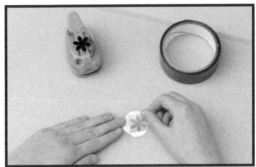

3 Complete the design by mounting a flower brad fastener (Provo Craft) at the center of each embellished flower.

Designing with pressed flowers

A sharp graphic layout is softened with the addition of real pressed flowers punched into a variety of square sizes. Follow the step shots on the next page to craft punched floral designs. Punch squares (Carl, EK Success, Emagination Crafts, Punch Bunch) from cardstock in shades of purple and soft yellow. Randomly layer squares on black border as shown; mount border on purple background. Double mat photos; punch small square design in top photo before matting. Offset and mount small photo squares on matting and background as shown. Hand letter title; shade with lavender chalk. Computer print journaling on gray paper; cut title and journaling blocks to size and double mat.

Torrey Miller, Photos Jodi Amidei

Out
of
Stone

One fairly cold winter day I found this hearty purple pansy growing strong, right out of a crack where the sidewalk meets the street in front of our house. It amazed me...to see such beauty growing out of stone.

"I'm always looking for new ways to use what I already have on hand. Combining punch art and pressed flowers breathes new life into both!"

-Torrey Miller

1 Mount pressed pansy atop white cardstock with liquid adhesive (Duncan) to strengthen the flower before punching. Use a scrap of cardstock to help slip glue underneath all petal edges to hold flower securely in place. Let dry completely.

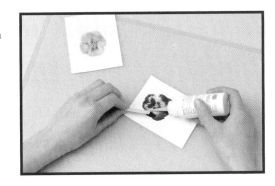

2 Flip square punches over to view area of flower to be punched. Punch two or three different sizes of squares into flower. Number the punched pieces on the back as you go; underline the numbered pieces so you can tell which side is right-side up (i.e, a 6 versus a 9) when reassembling.

3 Reassemble and mount punched squares into original flower design with self-adhesive foam spacers.

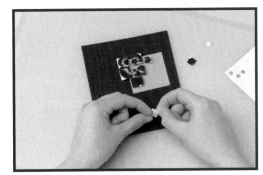

Coloring punch art with flowers

Once you've incorporated pressed flowers into your punch art, bloom into flower pounding—transferring floral pigments directly to paper. Simply layer newspaper with cardstock, a flower and then a paper towel. Pound the flower with a hammer to transfer the pigment to the paper, adjusting the force used as needed to darken the impression. Remove remaining flower pieces and pulp from cardstock with tweezers. Press backside of paper with a medium (no steam!) iron for 20 seconds to flatten.

Bright-colored, thin-petaled, single flowers work best. Try pansies, Johnny-jump-ups, forget-me-nots, coreopsis, daisies, impatiens, phlox, cosmos and verbena—even ferns—for glorious color results. Then punch the impression with your favorite floral or geometric-shaped punch. You'll never look at the flowers in your yard quite the same again!

Additional instructions & credits

Cover art

Punches used—Geraniums: five-flower corner punch (Family Treasures), gingko leaves (Paper Adventures). Daisies: small and large daisies (Marvy/Uchida), mini (Family Treasures), small (Marvy/Uchida) sun, ⅛" circle (Fiskars), small and large ash leaf (Punch Bunch). Tulips: teardrop (Paper Adventures), leaves (Family Treasures). Tiger Lilies: pistil and stamen shapes (Family Treasures), large kikyou's (Carl), stems and leaves (Family Treasures). Cherry Blossoms: birch leaves (Paper Adventures), large and jumbo fern leaves (Punch Bunch), small (EK Success) and medium (Emagination Crafts) ivy leaves, ⅛" circles. *Valerie Brincheck*

Title page art

Punches used—Border (Emagination Crafts), ¼" circles. Vase: leaf (Emagination Crafts), fern (Punch Bunch), swirl border (All Night Media). Telephone: small circle (McGill), ¹⁄₁₆" circles (McGill), square (McGill), swirl border (Family Treasures), ¼" circles, primitive heart (Emagination Crafts). Candle: ornament (Emagination Crafts), mini sun (Marvy/Uchida), jumbo circle, apple (Punch Bunch), primitive heart. *Kathleen Aho*

Bookplate art (page 3)

Punches used—Watering can (Punch Bunch), mini hearts (Fiskars), fern (Punch Bunch), ¹⁄₁₆" round punch. *Beverly Sizemore*

Introduction art (page 6)

Punches used—Leaves (Punch Bunch). *Michele Gerbrandt*

Photo contributors

Artist index

Contributing Memory Makers Masters

Sources

The following companies manufacture products featured in this book. Please check your local retailers to find these materials. In addition, we have made every attempt to properly credit the items mentioned in this book. We apologize to any company that we have listed incorrectly or the sources were unknown, and we would appreciate hearing from you.

3L Corp.
(800) 828-3130
www.3lcorp.com

Accu-Cut
(800) 288-1670
www.accucut.com

All My Memories
(888) 553-1998
www.allmymemories.com

All Night Media®, Inc.
(800) 782-6733

American Crafts
(800) 879-5185
www.americancrafts.com

American Tag Company
(800) 223-3956

American Tombow, Inc.
(800) 835-3232
www.tombowusa.com

Angelwings Enterprises
(800) 400-3717

ARTchix Studio
(250) 370-9985
www.artchixstudio.com

Artistic Wire Ltd.™
(630) 530-7567

Avant Card
www.avantcard.com

Beadery®, The/Greene
Plastics Corp.
(401) 539-2432

Biblical Impressions
(877) 587-0941
www.biblical.com

Blumenthal Lansing Company
(563) 538-4211

Bo-Bunny Press
(801) 771-4010
www.bobunny.com

Canson, Inc.®
(800) 628-9283

Carl Mfg. USA, Inc.
(800) 257-4771
www.carl-products.com

ChartPak
(800) 628-1910
www.chartpak.com

Close To My Heart®
(800) 655-6552
www.closetomyheart.com

Club Scrap™, Inc.
(888) 634-9100
www.clubscrap.com

C.M. Offray & Son, Inc.
www.offray.com

Colorbök™, Inc.
(800) 366-4660
www.colorbok.com

Colors By Design
(800) 832-8436
www.colorsbydesign.com

Copic
www.copicmarker.com

Craf-T Products
(507) 235-3996

Creative Imaginations
(800) 942-6487
www.cigift.com

Creative Impressions
(719) 577-4858
www.creativeimpressions.com

Cretacolor
(no contact info available)

C-Thru® Ruler Co., The
(800) 243-8419
www.cthruruler.com

Current® Inc.
(800) 848-2848
www.currentinc.com

Debbie Mumm®
(888) 819-2923
www.debbiemumm.com

Delta Technical Coatings, Inc.
(800) 423-4135

Design Originals
(800) 877-0067
www.d-originals.com

DMC Corp.
(973) 589-0606
www.dmc.com

DMD Industries, Inc.
(800) 805-9890
www.dmdind.com

Duncan Enterprises
(559) 294-3282

EK Success™ Ltd.
(800) 524-1349
www.eksuccess.com

Ellison® Craft & Design
(800) 253-2238
www.ellison.com

Emagination Crafts Inc.
(630) 833-9521
www.emaginationcrafts.com

Family Treasures, Inc.®
(800) 413-2645
www.familytreasures.com

Faux Memories
(813) 269-7946
www.fauxmemories.com

Fibers by the Yard
www.fibersbytheyard.com

Fiskars, Inc.
(800) 950-0203
www.fiskars.com

Frances Meyer, Inc.®
(800) 372-6237
www.francesmeyer.com

Funkie Ladiez
(303) 858-9950

Funky Frinjz
(303) 313-3814

Gifted Line, The
(800) 533-7263

Glue Dots® International
(wholesale only)
(888) 688-7131
www.gluedots.com

Halcraft USA, Inc.
(212) 276-1580

Hero Arts® Rubber
Stamps, Inc.
(800) 822-4376
www.heroarts.com

Hirschberg Schutz & Co., Inc.
(800) 221-8640

Hyglo®/AmericanPin
(800) 821-7125

Impress Rubber Stamps
(206) 901-9101
www.impressrubberstamps.
com

Jewel Craft LLC
(201) 223-0804
www.jewelcraft.biz

JudiKins
(310) 515-1115

K & Company
(888) 244-2083
www.kandcompany.com

Karen Foster Design
(801) 451-9779
www.karenfosterdesign.com

Keeping Memories Alive®
(800) 419-4949
www.keepingmemoriesalive.
com

Kolo™, Inc.
(888) 828-0367
www.kolo-usa.com

Kreinik Mfg. Co., Inc.
(800) 537-2166
www.kreinik.com

Lasting Impressions for
Paper, Inc.
(800) 936-2677

Loew Cornell
(201) 836-7070
www.loew-cornell.com

Magenta Rubber Stamps
(800) 565-5254
www.magentarubberstamps.
com

Magic Scraps™
(972) 385-1838
www.magicscraps.com

Making Memories
(800) 286-5263
www.makingmemories.com

Marvy® Uchida
(800) 541-5877
www.uchida.com

McGill Inc.
(800) 982-9884
www.mcgillinc.com

Mill Hill
www.millhill.com

Mrs. Grossman's Paper Co.
(800) 429-4549
www.mrsgrossmans.com

Nankong Enterprises, Inc.
(302) 731-2995
www.nankong.com

On The Surface
(847) 675-2520

Paper Adventures®
(800) 727-0699
www.paperadventures.com

Paper Garden, The
(210) 494-9602

Paper Loft, The
(801) 254-1961
www.paperloft.com

Plaid Enterprises, Inc.
(800) 842-4197
www.plaidonline.com

PrintWorks
(800) 854-6558

Provo Craft®
(888) 577-3545
www.provocraft.com

PSX Design™
(800) 782-6748
www.psxdesign.com

Punch Bunch, The
(254) 791-4209
www.thepunchbunch.com

Punch Studio
(310) 390-9900

QuicKutz
(888) 702-1146
www.quickutz.com

Quilters' Resource, Inc.
(800) 676-6543
www.quiltersresource.com

Ranger Industries, Inc.
(800) 244-2211
www.rangerink.com

Rubba Dub Dub
(707) 748-0929
www.artsanctum.com

Sanford® Corp.
(800) 323-0749
www.sanfordcorp.com

Scrap Ease®
(435) 645-0696

Scrap Pagerz™
(425) 645-0696
www.scrappagerz.com

Scrappin' Dreams
(417) 831-1882

Scratch-Art® Company, The
(800) 377-9003
www.scratchart.com

Serendipity Stamps
(816) 532-0740
www.serendipitystamps.com

Staedtler®, Inc.
(800) 927-7723
www.staedtler-usa.com

Stampa Rosa, Inc.
(800) 554-5755
www.stamparosa.com

Stampendous!®/Mark
Enterprises
(800) 869-0474
www.stampendous.com

Stampers Anonymous,
The Creative Block
(440) 333-7941
www.stampersanonymous.com

Stampin' Up!®
(800) 782-6787
www.stampinup.com

Stickopotamus®
(888) 270-4443
www.stickopotamus.com

Suze Weinberg Design
(732) 761-2400
www.schmoozewithsuze.com

Tie Me to the Moon™
(888) 509-2193
www.tiemetothemoon.com

Toner™ Plastics
(413) 789-1300
www.tonerplastics.com

Tsukineko®, Inc.
(800) 769-6633
www.tsukineko.com

Wintech International Corp.
(800) 263-6043
www.wintechint.com

Wonderland Emporium, Inc.
(800) 583-6041
www.wonderlandemporium.
com

Wordsworth
(719) 282-3495
www.wordsworthstamps.com

Ye Old Stamping Grounds
(406) 452-5880
www.yeoldestampinggrounds.
com

Punch guide

The punch shapes shown here and on pages 93, 94 and 95 are some of the ones used most frequently throughout this book and are shown for your reference. Not all punches used in projects are shown. Punch shapes are shown at 70% (shown at 100% on page 95) but may vary in size and shape by manufacturer.

Mega/giga punches

| circle | circle | square | decorative square | decorative square |

| rectangle | hexagon | scalloped heart | heart | chunky heart |

| squiggled heart | maple leaf | oak leaf | maple leaf | oak leaf |

| birch leaf | twig | five-petal flower | six-petal flower | nine-petal flower | daisy |

Jumbo and large punches

sunflower silhouette   pinecone   graphic pine tree   oak tree   pine tree   cactus

dragonfly   butterfly   snowflake   sailboat   watering can

mitten   bell   angel   light bulb   ornament   circle   circle

oval   square   square   decorative square   star   heart

heart   primitive heart   tree   holly leaf   doll   tooth   apple

Punch guide continued

Decorative corner, edger and frame punches

five-flower

lattice

pagoda silhouette

quilt

quilt

quilt

quilt

menorah

Japanese symbol

Egyptian eye

Medium punches

circle

circle

decorative square

sun

Star of David

heart

maple leaf

hawthorn leaf

grape leaf

oak leaf

maple leaf

ash leaf

birch leaf

flower

flower silhouette

eight-petal daisy

six-petal daisy

pompom

tree

tree

snowflake

snowflake

apple

fish

butterfly

shell

starfish

shell

fish

dragon

kokopelli

fleur-de-lis

squiggle or allegro

Small punches

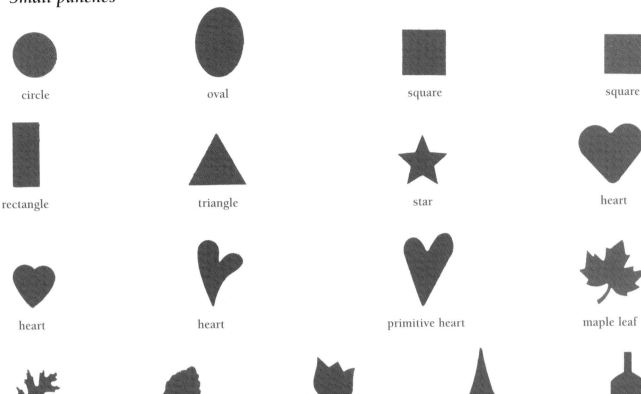

circle

oval

square

square

rectangle

triangle

star

heart

heart

heart

primitive heart

maple leaf

oak leaf

birch leaf

tulip

teardrop

dreidle

Mini and extended-reach punches

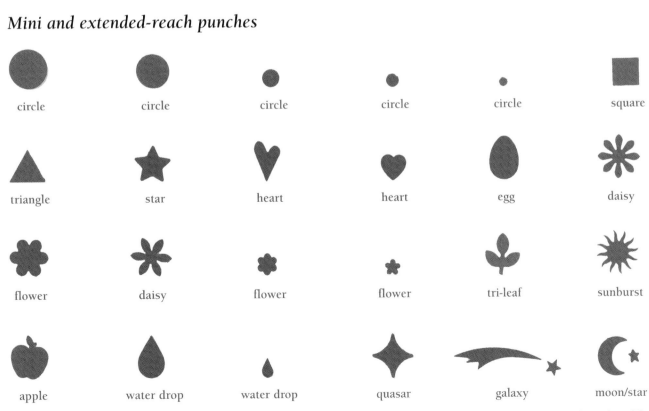

circle

circle

circle

circle

circle

square

triangle

star

heart

heart

egg

daisy

flower

daisy

flower

flower

tri-leaf

sunburst

apple

water drop

water drop

quasar

galaxy

moon/star

Index

If you liked the techniques featured in this book, you're going to love these other great Memory Makers books! Check for them at your local bookstore, craft store or on the Internet at www.memorymakersmagazine.com.